# A HOME

Inspiring and *heartfelt* tales of cat adoptions

ELAINE MARLIER

ILLUSTRATIONS BY JUDITH ANGELL MEYER

First Edition
January 2008



ISBN: 0-9800867-1-X

**Published in the United States of America by:**

DNJ Books
P.O. Box 620096
Littleton, Colorado 80162
Email: info@dnjbooks.com
Website: www.dnjbooks.com

**Designer**

Michele Renée Ledoux
www.mledoux.com

**Copy Editor**

Julia Wade Fliss
jfliss@artasendlesspossibility.com

FOR MELANIE –

# foreword

While there is nothing wrong with buying a cat—there is everything right with adopting one! The belief that cats in shelters are just unwanted animals and "never did have a home" is simply not true. Every cat in every shelter across America has a story to tell. Whether they came from a nice, loving home, were abused or neglected by their prior owners, or were found wandering lost in a field somewhere, they have a history. They were not *born* in the shelter. Even kittens who end up in shelters, although it may be a short one, still have a past.

While many of the cats found in shelters are mixed breeds, there are some shelters that provide temporary homes for purebreds. Animal shelters are like a used parking lot of cats. You can find almost every size, color and breed imaginable. Whatever your preference, there will undoubtedly be "a furry friend" to fit your bill. Unlike purchasing a used car that will hopefully give you years of dependable travel along the highways, adopting a cat from a shelter will net you a lifetime of adoring eyes, great companionship, laughter filled with lots of "scratchy" kisses, and the greatest pleasure of all—the capture of your heart.

As a connection between two souls, the benefits of adoption are twofold. For the animal, the benefit is profound. Simply stated—they know. They know that you are the one who took them from the shelter and gave them a home. They know you are the one who gave them that second chance. Although they cannot speak the words, they show their appreciation through the love and devotion they give you every day. For the human, the benefit is profound as well. There is a certain emotional satisfaction that comes from having a loving companion who exists solely due to the gracious, unselfish, wonderful deed a human has done by adopting. It is this inside joy of the heart that comes from giving an animal the opportunity for a new life.

*That* is the human-animal bond.

# why pets do not live as long as people

Being a veterinarian, I had been called to examine a twelve-year-old Siamese cat named Precious. The cat's owners, Brian, Lisa and their little girl, Eliza, were all very attached to Precious. They were praying for a miracle.

I examined Precious and found that she was dying of cancer. I told the family that unfortunately there were no miracles left for Precious, and offered to perform the euthanasia procedure for the old cat in the privacy of their home.

As we made the arrangements, Brian and Lisa told me they thought it would be good for six-year-old Eliza to observe the procedure. They felt it would help their daughter understand the cycle of life.

The next day, I felt the familiar catch in my throat as Precious' family surrounded her. Eliza seemed so calm as she petted the old cat for the last time that I had to question whether or not she understood what was going on. Within a few minutes, Precious slipped peacefully away and began her journey to Rainbow Bridge. Eliza seemed to accept the transition without any difficulty or confusion.

We all sat together for a while, holding hands, wondering aloud about the sad fact that animal lives are shorter than human lives.

Surprisingly, six-year-old Eliza, who had been listening quietly, spoke up, "I know why!"

Startled, we all turned to her. What came out of her mouth next stunned me. I'd never heard a more comforting explanation. These are the words she spoke:

"Everybody is born so that they can learn through their lifetime how to live a good life, like loving everyone else, and being nice, right?"

We all nodded in agreement.

"Well…animals already know how to do that when they're born…so they don't need to live as long!"

*Original author—Unknown*

## Table of Contents

**Author**
Elaine Marlier
www.dnjbooks.com

**Illustrator**
Judith Angell Meyer
www.fortmeyereditions.com

**Designer**
Michele Renée Ledoux
www.mledoux.com

**Editor**
Julia Wade Fliss
www.artasendlesspossibility.com

# broken tail kitty

## CHAPTER ONE

# broken tail kitty

## THE VALUE OF LOVE

Ashley appeared on Michelle's doorstep the minute she heard the news. A new family member had just arrived.

"Wow! She's gorgeous!"

"I named her Priscilla," Michelle boasted proudly. "I wanted a name that starts with a "P" because she is just like a princess...don't you think?"

Ashley reached over and stroked the soft, silky fur. A long, satisfied purr told her the gesture was welcome.

"You should tell your parents to buy you one, and then we'd both have kitties!"

Ashley slowly hung her head. She knew that wasn't possible. Michelle had told her on the phone how much her parents had paid for that kitten. From royalty or not, her parents simply didn't have that kind of money. Six hundred dollars would buy a lot of food for their household.

The entire afternoon the girls laughed and giggled while chasing Priscilla around the room, teasing her with her new toys. Michelle pointed out every single accessory they had purchased, giving a detailed explanation as to why she chose each piece. The pink, canopy bed, the fluffy, fur blanket, the rose-colored denim collar adorned with faux diamonds, and the three-story condominium were all shown off with pride. Ashley could only imagine that Michelle's parents had spent just as much on the accessories as they had on Priscilla.

Despite the differences in their parents' incomes—and social standing in the community—Ashley and Michelle were the best of friends. Their parents rarely interacted with each other, but afternoon playtime for the girls was an every day occurrence. Ashley had never been bothered by the fact that Michelle was always dressed in the latest designer fashions, had the newest games and electronic toys on the market, and had a coordinating bedroom ensemble that was fit for a magazine ad. She had never once been jealous that Michelle always got everything she asked for. She knew her parents did the best they could for her. They were always making sacrifices, always doing without so that she could have nice clothes to wear. Even with their modest income, they somehow always managed to buy the things that were most important to a nine-year-old girl. She was proud of that. She was proud of them.

Greg and Wendy were equally proud of their daughter. They were sure their belief—that Michelle's parents lavished her with material things to off-set the time they did not spend with her—was shared by their daughter. Ashley preferred family time. She would much rather spend the evening with them watching a movie and sharing a bowl of popcorn than be up in her room playing the latest video game—alone. Never once had she come home from Michelle's house asking for the things she had. She had always been perfectly content with what she had. The kitten, however, seemed to change things.

Afternoon playtime that was once shared between the two homes soon became a rare occurrence at their house. Michelle no longer came over; Ashley was always over at her house. Almost three months of constant chatter about Priscilla left Greg and Wendy realizing, for the first time, their daughter truly desired something Michelle had. It was evident. Ashley would never ask, but deep down inside, they knew. Knowing they could sacrifice just a little more, they knew what they had to do.

With Ashley in her classes at school, Greg and Wendy made a trip to the local humane society. Together they stood in awe at how many cats and kittens were available for adoption. Wendy's eyes scanned cage after cage, her heart breaking with every glance. She silently watched as people passed by the cages, some stopping to hold an animal, others merely looking as they walked by. Her attention was quickly captured by a small, white kitten with two small brown patches just over his ears. Each time someone passed by his kennel, he would get up, walk right up to the bars and rub his cheek firmly against them. Turning a complete circle, he would then sit down right at the front of the cage and purr. It almost seemed like he was asking someone to take him home. Wendy noticed though, that no one asked to hold him. No one even reached over to pet him on the head. Everyone that stopped simply looked at him, and then walked away.

"Do you see that?" She pointed over in his direction.

Greg's eyes followed the path of her finger.

"What?"

"That white kitten over there, no one has even petted him."

Wendy waited momentarily until the path was clear, and then headed straight for his cage with Greg following close behind her. Standing directly in front of him, the little white kitten stood up and performed his routine for her. Pressing his cheek against the bars, he slowly turned his complete circle. Wendy noticed that the patches over his ears matched a perfectly round circle of brown in the middle of his back and, instantly realized why no one had asked to see him. He only had half a tail. Although brown, like his ears and the circle on his back, his tail was short and bent at the end. He sat down in front of her and purred. Reaching over, Wendy rubbed the side of his cheek through the bars with her fingers.

"Would you like to hold him?" the voice seemed to carry with it a silent plea. A shelter volunteer had noticed the little kitten was finally getting some attention. She quickly appeared by Wendy's side.

"Actually yes, yes I would."

The little kitten instantly curled himself up into a ball in Wendy's arms. Snuggling close to her, he tilted his head backwards and stared straight up at her, directly into her eyes. He stretched one paw out across her left arm. His purr was soft and mellow. He seemed to be smiling.

Wendy slowly stroked his fur. "What happened to his tail?"

"We have no idea. Someone found him wandering the streets and brought him in."

"Do you know how old he is?"

"Not exactly. We're guessing he was about two months old when he came here…so he's probably around five months now."

Swaying the kitten gently back and forth, Wendy turned around and looked at her, "He's been here for three months?" Her surprise was clearly evident in her tone.

The volunteer shook her head, "It's sad, but yes. He's been here that long."

"How sad that no one has wanted him before," Wendy thought as she gently rocked the little kitten. He continued to purr.

"Has no one wanted him because of his tail?"

Not wanting to answer the question the volunteer simply raised her hands, acknowledging that she wasn't sure of the reason. Wendy, however, was.

Turning around to face her husband, she looked up at him with adoring eyes.

"Would you like to hold him sir?" The volunteer quickly interjected. She was now full of hope.

Glancing back at his wife, Greg smiled, "Do you want to look at some of the other kittens?"

Wendy only shook her head.

Turning his attention back to the volunteer, his words were soft, "I don't think I really need to. I think I'll have plenty of time to hold him at home."

Ashley had no idea why her parents were so elated or why they met her at the door when she returned home from school. Following them into the kitchen as she had been instructed to do, she watched their every movement. In the doorway Wendy stopped and pointed towards the corner. With an overwhelming sense of curiosity, Ashley's eyes followed along the edge of the wall in the direction her mother was pointing. Suddenly they froze. Off in the corner, next to the pantry, was an old yellow square pillow. Curled up on top of it, sleeping soundly, was a small white ball of fur.

"A kitty!" Her voice squealed with excitement. For months she had been secretly praying for a kitten and now, without even asking, she had one of her very own.

Running over to the corner, she quickly scooped the kitten up in her arms. That little spark of life that Greg and Wendy had watched slowly disappear since Priscilla's arrival was now shining brilliantly again in their daughter's eyes.

Hugging the kitty tightly to her face, Ashley twirled around in circles, freely giving the kisses she had so longed to give.

On the ride home from the shelter, Greg and Wendy had already discussed how they would address the issue of the kitten's broken tail with Ashley. They were both sure that she was mature enough to understand their choice. Knowing Michelle's kitten was flawless, they had no doubt their daughter was intelligent enough not to make comparisons between the two, and to understand the differences in their situations. They knew Ashley would understand the value of love. Sooner than they had anticipated, that discussion would take place. At dinner that evening, only several hours later, they were given the opportunity to give their speech.

"Mom, why does our kitten have a broken tail?"

Glancing over at her, Wendy smiled, "We don't know the answer to that honey. We think that he might have been abandoned by someone. No one really knows what his past is. All we know is that he desperately needed a home with a lot of love, and that we can definitely provide for him."

Ashley looked down at her plate, "He's really pretty, but his tail doesn't look at all like Priscilla's tail. Hers is long and slinky, and it doesn't have a kink in it. Hers is perfect."

Wendy was absolutely shocked by her statement. The daughter who she knew would never make such a comparison and never make a statement comparing the unfortunate against the fortunate, had just done the one thing that they were positive they had taught her never to do.

"Honey, you cannot compare this kitten to Michelle's. Her parents paid a lot of money for that "perfect tail." We did something far better than just giving a kitten a home—we gave a kitten that desperately needed it…a second chance at life."

Ashley again looked down at her plate, "I know….but didn't the shelter have any kittens with normal tails?"

Wendy set down her fork on the table and stared directly at her daughter. She had been prepared for this conversation, but she had not been prepared for that question.

"Yes Ashley…they did! They had a lot of cats and kittens with perfect tails!" Her tone clearly held a hint of anger.

"We chose him, Ashley, for that very reason…because his tail was broken. There were lots of cats up for adoption, but that very mentality is what caused no one to want him! He had been in that shelter for almost three months—three months due to the fact that he wasn't perfect!"

Ashley looked up at her mother. She remained very silent.

Wendy continued, "You know, Ashley…I am very disappointed in you. We have always taught you that love is more important than beauty. It's not what you have in life…but what you give. In time, I know you will see that you are going to get much more from this kitten than you could ever get from a "perfect" kitten. He knows…trust me he knows. He knows we did not care about his tail…he knows that he was in need of a good, loving home, a home that could forgive his imperfections, and that….we can give him! For that, he will be forever grateful. You simply cannot get a more special bond than that!"

Ashley would soon discover just how true her mother's words were.

Just as she was about to fall asleep for the evening, she suddenly felt something rub up against her cheek. Rolling over, she sat straight up. A soft, mellow "meow" echoed throughout the air. Leaning over on her pillow, she propped herself up on one elbow. She was face to face with the broken tail kitty. Reaching over, she gently stroked his fur. His hind legs bending down, he turned a half circle. The broken tail stared her directly in the face. Slowly, she permitted her hand to gently slide down every short inch of it. His head turned back, arched over his shoulders, and he stared directly into her eyes. She thought he seemed to smile. Suddenly, she felt the guilt.

"How is it little boy…that I can turn my back on you because of an imperfection…and yet you are right here by my side?"

The broken tail kitty curled himself up into a ball and laid down next to her. He let out a long, content purr. Ashley gently stroked his fur as she slowly drifted off to sleep.

Once again, it was a kitten that brought about a change to the normal household routine; however this time, the change was welcomed by Greg and Wendy. Ashley hardly ever left the house anymore after school to go to Michelle's. Now it was the opposite—Michelle was always at their home. The girls would spend hours up in Ashley's room playing with Bee Tee, sometimes known as Bee for short. An odd name for a cat, Ashley had chosen it proudly. A defect once scorned now supplied the initials for a name—Broken Tail. With Bee Tee and Priscilla both at around the same age, Bee Tee had completely taken over. He now held center stage.

Wendy could not hold back her tears when she passed by the open door to Ashley's room one afternoon and accidentally overheard the conversation between the two girls.

"Gosh Ashley, I so wish Priscilla was more like Bee Tee. He simply adores you! He is always following you everywhere you go! He constantly wants to play and snuggle! He is just sooooo loving!"

Ashley led the ball that was attached to a string across the floor. Bee Tee hunched down and prepared himself to launch.

"But Priscilla does that too, doesn't she?"

"Not anymore she doesn't. She doesn't like to do anything but prance around the house all day and look pretty. She's always just hanging out in her bed or her condo. She doesn't even like for you to hold her anymore!"

Ashley glanced down at Bee Tee. He had succeeded in catching the ball. With it firmly in his mouth, he rolled over and stretched out one paw, placing it directly on top of her knee. A soft, faint, muffled purr could be heard. She gently rubbed the fur on his head.

"I don't think Bee Tee will ever change. I think he will always be this loving. My mom says that he knows we saved him—that he will always know that we were the ones who gave him a second chance at life when no one else wanted him. I really do believe that. I think his gratitude will stay with him forever."

Staring deeply into his eyes, she scratched him behind his ears, "Huh boy?"

This time, she was sure he smiled.

# tasha and her kittens

CHAPTER TWO

# lives lost

The old house was suddenly quiet. There was no movement. Tasha listened intently. She had to make sure no one was there before venturing up the stairs. She had no idea there would no longer be any movement above her. Slowly creeping up the stairs, she poked her head through the doorway. Peering from around the corner, the space was empty. Fear entered her mind with every step. She worried about her kittens down in the basement. She could not let anyone find out they were there. Cautiously entering the kitchen, her fear slowly subsided. No one was around. She scrambled to find whatever food she could. There wasn't much, but whoever abandoned the house at least left some things. It would be enough to sustain her, at least until the kittens were older. She knew eventually they would have to find another home, but for now, this one would have to suffice.

Tasha came to know the house well. It took several days for her to understand she could come and go freely up the stairs, and then back down to the basement, without the fear of being seen. She didn't understand the word abandon, but she now realized there were no longer humans around. There was no longer a threat to her kittens. For weeks she had the freedom of the entire house, but her loving, nurturing nature would not allow her to partake in that freedom. She only permitted herself to leave the basement long enough to search for food, and then she returned as quickly as possible to supervise her young.

With the kittens almost eight weeks old, food was now very scarce. Tasha knew it was time for her to venture back out into the world. The kittens would need more than her milk. She would need food for herself. She knew she had lost several pounds—she could feel her own lightness—she just wasn't sure how many "several" were.

Early in the morning Tasha stared up at the window. She could see the sunlight pouring in. Knowing this was the day she would have to leave the house, her route was already planned. A table just to the side of the window would give her the height she needed to make it to the window sill. From there, it was just a slight slide out the crack in the window. The kittens would be safe in the basement. For almost two months no one had bothered them. No one had even known they were there. With one flying leap she was on the table. Her paws walked close to the edge, her eyes remained fixed on her kittens. They were all sound asleep, curled up together in one massive ball in the corner. Stopping just short of the edge, her eyes floated up to the window sill. She squinted at the sunlight. Sitting down she kept her head tilted upwards. She looked back at her kittens, and then turned and faced the window again. In one split second she was on the sill. She edged her way through the crack. Suddenly she was outside.

Sitting perfectly still in the grass, Tasha surveyed the surroundings. The sun warmed her entire body. She hadn't felt that kind of warmth in months. Trying hard to stare up at the sun, all she could do was squint. It was far too bright. She could see the tall, city buildings off in the distance. She knew she would be able to find food on the city streets, but they were too far away. She didn't want to leave her kittens for that length of time. Deciding to walk towards the trees, she slowly got up and headed north.

# as they watched

Snowball rolled over, bumping up against Tommy.

*Tommy…hey, Tommy. I think mom just left us!*

Poking his head from underneath his paw, Tommy rolled his eyes. *What are you talking about? Mom would never leave us!*

*She just did.*

*She probably went upstairs to get food, go back to sleep.*

*No Tommy, really…she just disappeared through that box up there on the wall! I watched her leave!*

Tommy instantly woke up. He flipped his body over and found himself lying across Snowball's back, looking towards the window. Intertwined in that manner, the two of them almost resembled a jigsaw puzzle. It was obvious to anyone who saw them that they certainly had to be related. The two of them definitely resembled their tuxedo mother as well. Tommy was solid black, sporting two white circles on his body—one on his head at the base of his right ear, the other near his left hind leg. Snowball's solid white body was adorned with two patches of black fur—one at the base of her left ear, the other encircling her right hind leg and drifting partially up her tail. Aside from the differences in their paws, the two were exact opposites.

Lily put her tiny claws into the wood, pulling herself up directly next to Snowball. A small meow echoed throughout the basement.

*Mom left us? What do you mean?*

Tommy was still staring at the window. Smokie pushed hard up against Tommy's back.

*You don't think Snowball is right, do you Tommy? You don't think mom left us—right?*

*I don't know. She's always gone up those stairs over there when she's left us alone. She's never even been near that box. I don't know where she would have gone!*

With all four of them staring up at the window, they curled together tightly for security. Their small bodies would not allow them to stare for very long. Almost in unison, they drifted back off to sleep.

Smokie was the first to awake. He peered around the room. It was completely silent. Edging himself out from underneath the balls of fur, he got up and walked over to the stairs. Sitting down directly in front of them, he stared up at the door at the top. It was partially ajar.

*Mom? Mom are you up there?*

His cries awoke his siblings. Joining him at the bottom of the stairs, they all sat and looked up at the door.

*Let's go look for her up there.*

*I told you guys she's not up there. I watched her leave through that box on the wall.*

They all focused their attention back to the window Snowball referenced.

*What do you think is out there?*

*I don't know. That light is awfully bright though…whatever it is, it can't hurt us down here. You saw it, it's like it's trying to come in, but the wall keeps blocking it.*

*Yeah you're right Tommy. We're safe down here.*

Even though all of the kittens were the same age—Tommy seemed to be the oldest. His siblings looked up to his wisdom. For Snowball, he was definitely her favorite. She loved Smokie and Lily just as much, but with Tommy, there was a stronger bond. There was something special about him. Maybe it was their shared looks that made her feel so close to him.

With the kittens back in their usual corner, Smokie couldn't shake the feeling that they would not see their mother again. He stared up at the window, leaning hard on Tommy's words. *That light can't hurt us down here.* Suddenly he nudged Tommy on the back of the head.

*Tommy, if that light is harmful…and mom's out there…*

*Lily perked up, He's right! What if that light can hurt mom?*

The four of them suddenly sat straight up. Instantly they knew what they had to do. They had to venture out to find their mother.

*Okay…let's be calm. Let's think. How are we going to get up there?*

Snowball had the answer—*That table. That's how mom got out. She jumped up on the table, and then jumped up on the ledge of the box.*

*Lily stared at the table. Do you think we can do it? It looks really high.*

*We can do it,* Tommy assured her. *Come on!*

With the consecutive order already in place, Tommy was the first to go. His fearless attitude assisted him with one quick leap, and then another. Standing on the sill, he turned around to face his siblings.

*It was easy, come on.*

Snowball quickly followed suit. The two of them stood on the ledge.

*There's not enough room for three of us up there.* Smokie stood staring at Tommy and Snowball.

*Okay. Snowy, go out the crack and wait. Don't go anywhere, just sit and wait for the rest of us.*

Snowball did as she was instructed. Sitting outside on the grass she had very mixed emotions. She had never seen such a wide open space. She was fearful of what lie ahead, but she loved the feel of the grass. It was so much softer than the old wooden floor she was accustomed to. She closed her eyes to shield out the sun. Her entire body reveled in warmth.

With only Tommy on the ledge, Smokie took one long leap to the table. He sat for a brief moment to enjoy his accomplishment.

*Come on Smokie.*

With Tommy's encouragement he quickly joined him on the sill, and then slipped through the crack in the window. All that remained was Lily.

*Come on Lily…you can do this.*

*No I can't. It's way too high!*

*Just back up a couple of steps and get a running start. You'll see. You can make it.*

Lily sat perfectly still, trembling inside. She wasn't sure if she was scared of the height, scared that she couldn't make it, or scared of what lie on the other side of the window. She could see the sunlight pouring in, but she had no desire to get any closer to it.

*You guys just go ahead. I'll stay here and wait for mom in case she comes back.*

*No Lily, we are all sticking together. We are not going to leave each other. Just take a couple of steps back and then go for it!*

Lily still hesitated, but she did have faith in her brother's words. Slowly she turned around and walked back about five steps. Stopping, she turned back around and sat down.

*Come on Lily!*

Staring hard into Tommy's eyes, she could see his pleas of encouragement. Without giving another thought to the endeavor, she stood up and charged at the table. In one flying leap she landed on all four paws.

*See…I told you that you could do it. Now come on, one more time.*

Now confident, she leaped again into the air, landing on the sill. Pausing briefly to smile at him, she then nudged her way through the crack. Tommy followed right behind her.

The four of them sat on the grass in awe. They had a mission, but none of them could move. The warmth of the sun beating down on them gave them a wonderful, peaceful sensation. Their fear of the bright light quickly dissipated. Although she was the last to arrive, Lily was the first to move. Darting straight ahead she ran, sinking her paws into the ground. Only ten feet away she stopped and rolled around in the grass.

*This is soooo much fun!*

Tommy looked at Snowball who then looked at Smokie. They all smiled at each other, and then quickly joined Lily in her task. Mission quickly forgotten, a new lesson was learned—how to play and have fun.

The chasing, running and playing lasted for only an hour, but it also lasted almost a half mile of distance. Totally overwhelmed by the fun, none of them realized how far they had traveled. They could no longer see the old abandoned house. The four of them sat among the tall trees in the wooded area. Snowball, Smokie and Lily all looked to Tommy for direction.

*Oh my gosh, Tommy. We don't know where we are, do we?*

*No Snowball, unfortunately we don't.*

None of them blamed Lily. They had all participated in the fun, and they had all enjoyed it immensely. They had no regrets, but now was the time to get serious. There was another mission at hand now—not to search for their mother, but to figure out how to get back to the safety of the house. None of them had any idea which direction they should go. They were lost. They all began to walk, following Tommy's lead, unknowingly, deeper into the wooded area, away from the house they sought.

Night time quickly approached. That beautiful, bright light faded away. All of them were scared, although Tommy could not admit it. He had to remain the strong one. Curling up together, they shielded themselves from the outside world underneath the darkness of a bush. Within minutes they had all drifted off to sleep. Their adventures had left them worn and tired. It would be the next morning before they awoke.

Snowball peered through one eye. The bright light had returned. She looked out beyond the bush, and then slowly closed her eye again. Extending out one paw, she hit Smokie right in the face.

*Hey…Snowball, watch it!*

Tommy opened his eyes. He looked over at Snowball. Her eyes were completely closed. Glancing over at Smokie, he then turned his attention towards where Lily should have been. Quickly he looked back at Smokie, then back again at Snowball. Suddenly he sat straight up. His eyes scanned the area.

*Hey! Where's Lily? Guys wake up! Where's Lily?*

Everyone opened their eyes. Panic immediately set in. Frantically they all began to search the area. Smokie was the first to jump up and begin to wander. Tommy and Snowball followed his lead.

*Lily! Lily! Where are you?*

Fear began to set in. The three of them continued to search, taking great care to keep each other in sight. For almost an hour their search continued through the wooded area, but all of their efforts were in vain. Lily was gone. Gathering back together underneath a tall tree, the three of them sat devastated, in silence.

Smokie finally spoke, *Where could she have gone?*

*I don't know, Smokie.* Tommy instantly felt the guilt. He should have kept a better eye on her. He knew how scared she had been to leave the basement, but he had forced her to. He suddenly wished he had allowed her to do as she wanted, to stay home and wait for their mother's return. He hung his head low. Snowball understood his thoughts.

*It's not your fault Tommy. We were supposed to stick together, she knew that.*

Tommy looked over at her. He appreciated her words, but nonetheless, had he allowed her to stay at the house, she wouldn't be lost. The three of them made an instant pact. They would begin their search again for her and for their mother, but they would not, under any circumstances, separate.

Their morning's travel took them outside the wooded area. With the trees now totally behind them, the path ahead gave no security at all. A huge shopping center lay in their view. No sign of Lily, or their mother, but there were hundreds of two-legged creatures moving swiftly back and forth from car to store.

*Where do we go from here, Tommy?*

*I don't know Snowball, but we have to stay away from them. We don't know who they are or what they'll do. Let's just sit here until I can think of a plan.*

*I'm really hungry.*

*So are we, Smokie. Don't worry, we'll find something to eat soon.*

Sitting behind a small concrete wall, the three of them quietly watched the people hurriedly walk back and forth, passing before them. One young woman caught Smokie's eye. It was almost as if he could see right through the white plastic sack she was carrying. He was sure he could smell the food—the food that was meant especially for them. Watching her every movement as she exited the store heading for her car, he thought for a brief moment that if he darted out in front of her, it would startle her just enough to cause her to drop the bag. Suddenly he could envision tiny kibbles scattered all over the ground. There would be plenty of food for the three of them. The mere thought of food caused his stomach to ache. Keeping his eyes affixed on the woman, he knew Tommy would not approve of his actions, but he also knew that he and Snowball had to be just as hungry as he was. There was no indication that they would ever find any food given their current situation. It was worth it—for him and his siblings. They had to eat. He had to do it. Not even glancing Tommy's way, with one flying leap he darted out in front of the woman. Just as he had anticipated, she flung her hands up in the air, dropping the bag on the pavement. Smokie kept on running, across the parking lot to the next row of cars before ducking down and hiding underneath a front tire. Lying there he stared at the cat food that was scattered down by her feet. He had been successful. The woman quickly looked around before bending down and picking up her bag. Smokie no longer watched her as she got into her car, backed up and drove away. His eyes remained affixed on the food.

Smokie would not even look in Tommy and Snowball's direction even though he knew they were watching him. Tommy was sure to scorn him. He would have to wait until after they had eaten to receive any approval for his heroic deed. With hunger pains tearing away at his stomach, not giving any thought to that which still surrounded him, he immediately darted out from underneath the car and ran towards the food. With his intently focused eyes, he never saw the car coming.

Tommy and Snowball watched in horror as Smokie lay on the payment.

*Smokieeeee……no!*

Their eyes could not believe what they were seeing. Tommy wanted desperately to run over to him but within seconds there were people flocked around him. One woman was standing up, a piece of paper and pen in her hands, squinting at the back of the car as it sped out of the parking lot.

*Is he okay Tommy? Please tell me Smokie is okay.*

*I don't know Snowball, I can't see anything.*

Suddenly all of the people stood up and began to disperse. No one seemed to go in the same direction. Snowball looked over at the spot where Smokie had been laying. He was no longer there.

*Where did he go Tommy?*

Snowball was completely devastated. It was hard enough watching him get hit, but to have him then disappear, that was more that she could handle.

*I don't know Snowy…One of those people must have taken him.*

*But why would they take him?*

Tommy looked at her with sad eyes. *I just don't know Snowy... let's hope it was so they could help him.*

Tommy and Snowball backed up and crouched down behind the wall. Huddled together they remained very still. They would wait there until darkness fell upon them before venturing out again.

*Do you think he's still alive Tommy?* The sadness they shared was clear in her voice.

*I don't know Snowy...I just don't know.*

Tommy stood guard while Snowball closed her eyes. He had no idea how many hours had passed before the darkness finally fell upon them. He listened with cautious ears, until there was no longer a sound around them. His eyes scanned the area, searching for any kind of movement. There was none. Snowball suddenly awoke with the movement of his body.

*I think everyone is gone Snowy. I see nothing. You wait right here, I'm going to go and see if the food is still on the ground.*

*No Tommy, I want to go with you.*

*Snowball—No! You saw what happened to Smokie. If it happens again—if it happens to me—I would never forgive myself for not having protected you...like I didn't protect Lily. Stay here, I'll let you know when the coast is clear.*

Tommy would not hear any objections. He ventured ahead alone, stopping just long enough to ensure Snowball had stayed in her place. Stretching his paws out onto the pavement, the smell attracted him to the spot where the food still lay. Walking with extreme caution he approached it. Looking to the left, then to the right there was no movement. There was nothing.

*Okay, Snowy...come on. The coast is clear.*

Snowball quickly approached his side.

*Hmmmm...food! This is sooooo good! I am so hungry!*

Within only minutes, the two of them had cleared the pavement, erasing all remnants of evidence of the sacrifice Smokie had made. With two full bellies, Tommy and Snowball turned in the direction of the wooded area they had left behind. It was time to begin their venture. They would walk until they found a safe, secure place to rest for the night. When daylight approached they would resume the journey to hopefully find their way back home.

The sunlight struck Tommy right in the eyes. Even with his lids closed, he knew it was morning. He sat up and began to think. Before Snowball awoke, he had devised a plan.

*Okay Snowy, I know what we're going to do.* He was looking out from the trees straight ahead, eyeballing a path directly in front of them. *We came from that direction—I'm sure of it. If we just try to backtrack, follow back the path that led us here...we should find the house.*

Snowball curled up her little, pink nose. Glancing around at the trees that surrounded them, she felt uneasy about the path. She did not share Tommy's assuredness about the direction. She did have to admit to herself though; he had led them back to the wooded area. He had been right about that. She stared ahead at the path, and then gave one last glance around the trees. Stretching out her paws, she stood up, taking her place next to her brother.

*Okay Tommy…I'm ready!*

With their eyes wide open and fixed straight ahead, they set out to face the day.

It took almost half of the day for the two of them to reach the other side of the woods. Peering out from behind a bush, Tommy noticed a wide open area in front of them. He stopped, staring straight ahead.

*Snowy…I think this is it! I think this is the way we came.*

*Are you sure Tommy? Are you sure?*

*I remember walking across a field like that before we got lost.*

Tommy's eyes first looked to the left, and then to the right. There was no sign of anyone, no movements of any kind. Taking a step out into the open field, Snowball followed his lead without hesitation.

A sense of peace quickly edged its way into Snowball's heart. With her first steps out into the open field, she remembered the sensation she felt on her paws the day when she first slipped through the crack in the window. Her very first touch of grass. That same sensation now lingered in her legs. Instantly she knew Tommy was right. They were heading in the right direction. They were in the right field. The sky was a royal shade of blue, painted only by white, soft blankets of clouds. The sun warmed the jaded blades of green beneath her paws. In her heart she knew, as the two of them walked side by side, they were going to find the house.

Before long, Tommy suddenly stopped dead in his tracks. Following suit, Snowball turned to face him.

*Snowball! Look straight ahead! The house! That's the house!*

Focusing her attention straight ahead, the house was distant, but in plain view. Tommy broke into an immediate sprint with Snowball right on his heals. The house came closer and closer into view. Tommy squinted hard to make out the vision he thought he saw. *Could it be? Could it really be?* His speed increased rapidly. Clearer and clearer the vision became.

*MOM!*

Just outside the small window, sitting as still as a statue, was Tasha. She was in the exact same spot she had been in ever since her return to the house—ever since she made the discovery that her kittens were gone.

*TOMMY! SNOWBALL! Where have you been?* Before an answer could be given, she looked to her left, and then to her right. Focusing her attention out amongst the open area, her eyes saw no more. Her joy was quickly crippled by sadness. *Where are Smokie and Lily?*

Tommy held his head low. He knew she would not blame him, but his guilt was still present. He still blamed himself.

*We don't know where Lily is. We all got lost in the wooded area. She just ventured out by herself. We searched and searched, but we just couldn't find her.*

*It's not his fault mom; Lily knew she was supposed to stay with us. She knew we were supposed to stick together.*

Tasha could sense their guilt. The look in her eyes proved she passed no judgment.

*What happened to Smokie?*

This time Snowball lowered her head. Visions of him lying on the pavement flashed before her eyes. *Smokie got hit by a car mom. He did it for us; he was just trying to get food. We were all so hungry.*

Tasha looked down at the two of them. As much as it pained her heart that two of her kittens had not returned, she could only show happiness for the two that stood before her.

*Come on you two, we have to find a new place to live. We can't stay in this house any longer. There's nothing left for us here.*

Tommy and Snowball knew their mother was right. Without Smokie and Lily, there was nothing left for them there.

# lily

## SCARED AND ALONE

Lily watched in total shock from underneath a car, only two rows over from where Smokie lay on the pavement. She had seen him the minute he darted out in front of the woman. She hadn't seen Tommy or Snowball, but she knew they had to be close by. She didn't mean to get lost, she had only wanted food. Thinking she had only walked some twenty feet or so, she turned back around, and the three of them were nowhere to be found. At first her mind flashed scenes of them walking the other direction, turning their back on her, but her heart would not allow that thought to truly process. She knew they loved her, even if she was the unconfident one of the bunch. They would never have walked away and left her behind. She simply got lost.

All of her thoughts of being scared and alone underneath that car had been immediately shattered by devastation in that one horrific moment when she first saw Smokie. Watching Smokie get hit by that car, her own self-concern instantly disappeared. She knew her siblings had to be right around the corner, probably witnessing the exact same thing she did, but her state of shock would not allow her to move. She was frozen. With wide eyes she watched her brother lying perfectly still, then just as Tommy and Snowball, she watched him disappear with a crowd of people. She too was left to wonder what would become of his fate. Crunched up behind the front tire she began to panic as the people walking by started to get closer to her. Someone could spot her; someone could take her away just like they had Smokie. Then she would never have a chance of finding Tommy and Snowball. She needed a new place to hide. Waiting for just the right opportunity, she quickly darted out from underneath the car, running as fast as she could to the back of a building. Walking around a big dumpster, she brushed her cheek up against its side. Finally, she had found peace and quiet. Curling up into a ball, she lay down behind it and slowly drifted off to sleep.

As night fell, Lily had absolutely no idea that Tommy and Snowball were in that very same parking lot, just around the front of the building, finally getting to eat. She could have been reunited, but she was too scared to venture out into the stillness of the eve. Tilting her nose up in the air, she leaped up into the dumpster to rummage for food. Thankfully there was enough there to sustain her. Peering her head up slowly from the dumpster, she surveyed the surroundings, then jumped out and curled back up behind it to face the darkness of the night. When daylight returned, she would feast again, and then gather up the strength and courage she needed to go out and search for her siblings. Fate however, had a different plan in store for her.

With the first ray of light shinning in her eyes, so too was the first sound of a human voice to her ears.

"Lynn…come out here!"

Joe had been taking empty boxes out to the dumpster when his eyes caught the first sight of a paw sticking out from behind the metal green wall. At six o'clock in the morning, that was the last thing he had expected to see.

"What? What is it?" Lynn appeared right by his side.

Joe shut the lid and walked around to the back of the dumpster. Lynn followed him.

"It's a kitten. Look at this…it's a kitten."

Lynn bent down and tried to stroke her, but Lily edged herself back further. Lynn could not squeeze between the dumpster and the concrete wall that surrounded it. "I wonder how she got out here?"

Lily permitted herself only a slight purr. She was in need of help, but she didn't want to appear overly anxious. She had no idea what their intentions were.

Joe bent down and pressed his face against the concrete. Stretching one arm out as far as he could, he reached between the wall and the dumpster, "I think I can reach it, if I can just get my arm back there far enough…"

His first effort failed. It took three attempts before he finally latched onto Lily's front leg. Gently he pulled her across the ground. Trying to show resistance, Lily allowed herself to be picked up. Joe pulled her tightly to his chest.

"Aw...what are you doing out here, little one?"

His voice was kind, his touch was soothing. Lily looked straight up into his eyes.

"She can't be more than nine or ten weeks old!" Lynn reached over and petted her on top of her head,"She is adorable."

Joe lifted her straight up into the air for inspection, then pulled her back against him,"Yep, she's a girl alright."

"How do you think she got way out here?"

"I don't know, but we certainly can't leave her here."

Joe smiled as he lifted Lily up, pressing her against his cheek,"Come on little girl, let's get you inside."

That afternoon Lily rode home curled up on Joe's lap, just underneath the steering wheel. She had no idea what was happening, but she felt a certain sense of security with him. Her initial apprehension had slowly begun to fade earlier in the day when he re-entered the office he had placed her in bearing food and water. Sitting in the corner, not permitting herself to be enticed, she watched him set the two bowls down on the floor. He spoke to her softly and then disappeared. To ensure her safety, she stared at the closed door for a long time before venturing over to the food bowl. Having eaten with a constant eye on the door, she then returned to her corner and curled up into a ball. Closing her eyes she felt a sense of relief, realizing the food and water had been hers for free. The giver had wanted nothing in return.

Joe hurriedly carried Lily into his apartment, holding her just under the tail of his shirt. He could not allow any of his neighbors to see her. The apartment complex he lived in did not allow pets of any kind; it was crucial she remain hidden. Once inside, he placed the bag on the counter and then gently set her down on the floor. Lily stood momentarily still. She wanted to run and hide, but in the back of her mind, she somehow knew the man wasn't going to hurt her. Slowly she put one paw forward, then turned around and looked up at Joe.

"Go ahead little girl. Go explore. It's okay."

Lily turned back around and walked straight into the living room. Surveying her new surroundings, she never noticed Joe quietly disappear into the kitchen. When he returned, he had a bowl of food, a bowl of fresh water, and a litter box, which was something she had never seen before.

The two of them were sitting on the couch in the living room that evening, curled up next to each other, when Pam walked in the door. Setting her purse down, she immediately noticed the litter pan in the hallway. Tilting her head sideways, she walked directly over to it and stared.

"Joe?"

"I'm in here."

Following the trail of his voice, she stopped on the other side of the coffee table. Lily looked up at her. Joe simply smiled.

"Joe…why is there a kitten on your sofa?"

Pam could easily see the gleam in his eyes as Joe told her of the dumpster rescue. She had always known he had a fondness for cats, but she had never actually seen him with one. Listening to his tale, she noticed how he constantly stroked Lily's fur. Something seemed to stir in the air. There seemed to be a new fondness in his voice.

"Isn't she just the cutest thing?"

Pam walked around the table and sat down next to him.

"She is Joe; she really is....but you know...you can't keep her."

Joe looked down at Lily with sad eyes. "I know Pam. I'll take her to the humane society in the morning. Tonight I just want to give her a warm, loving place to sleep."

# lily

## THE ADOPTION

Lily lay in her kennel, meowing at everyone in sight. She didn't want to be there. Desperately missing her siblings and her mother, she now found herself missing Joe. In those short, few days she thought she had actually found in him a person who would take care of her forever. She had allowed herself to become attached to him.

For someone who had no intention of keeping her, Joe had certainly showered her with a lot of gifts—and a lot of love. Her own personal bed lay next to his. Her food and water dish had their place in the kitchen, and her toys were scattered all throughout his apartment. In the mornings, Lily would follow Joe from room to room, listening to his soft voice as he continually spoke to her. Every night when he returned home from work, the two of them would roll around on the floor and chase balls back and forth. After dinner, she would lay next to him on the couch, curled up tightly against his leg while he gently stroked her fur. She didn't know the woman who kept coming over every night very well, but she didn't think she liked her much. She may have sat on the couch with them and petted her, but Lily could sense the friction. Every time she was there, she and Joe would have an intense conversation. Lily knew those conversations were about her. Now, lying alone in her kennel, she reflected back on the words she didn't want to remember.

"Joe…why is this kitten still here? The night you brought her home you said you were taking her to the shelter the very next morning…"

"I know Pam, I know. I'm going to take her…it's just…well it's just that she's so darn cute…and I really think she likes me."

"She may like you, but you know you cannot have pets here. All you need is to get caught with her and have to pay a fine…or better yet…get kicked out of here. You are not in a financial position to move right now. The longer you prolong this, the harder it is going to be."

"I know, I know. I'll take her down in the morning."

That same conversation, with only minor variations, occurred six nights in a row. Finally, on Saturday morning, Joe forced himself to let go. He knew Pam was right—he couldn't afford to get caught with Lily in the apartment. The final words of their nightly conversation struck him hard—it was going to be extremely difficult on him to give her up. He had already become very attached to her.

With Pam sitting in the car, Joe hesitantly got out, wrapping Lily up in his arms. Silently she watched through the windshield as he slowly walked along the concrete path, his head staring down at the bundle in his arms. She knew he did not want to give her up, but she had no idea how hard it was going to affect him—not until he appeared again in the doorway of the shelter—but without Lily in his arms. His face carried a look of total devastation. Instantly she felt his pain. Never, in all the time they had been dating, had she seen him so distraught. Her heart went out to him.

Pam felt sure the arts festival that afternoon would help to change Joe's spirit, but her assuredness was quickly dampened. His mood remained somber the entire day, his smile, hidden. Her weekend-long creative efforts to help ease his pain were in vain as well. Nothing seemed to work. No matter how hard she tried, she simply could not light a spark in his eyes.

It didn't take Pam long to realize that the regular work week routine was not going to help in fading away the memories of Lily. Her bed still remained next to Joe's. Her toys were gathered together and placed in a basket near the dining room table. A picture of her that Joe had shot with his cell phone was now framed and sitting on the fireplace mantel. His demeanor may have returned, but his spirit was still broken. Throughout the week she continually witnessed his many moments of drifted thoughts. Staring out the window or glancing up at Lily's picture, his conversation would abruptly stop, allowing silence to take over. She could not bear to see his sadness any longer. Knowing her parents would not object to her having a kitten in the townhouse she rented from them, Pam knew what she had to do.

Saturday morning Pam sat in her car, just outside the humane society watching their front doors. When they finally opened, she was the first one inside. Slowly walking down the rows of kennels, she was steadfast in her search. One by one her heart sank a little deeper with each tiny face she passed. Not ever having been to a shelter before, she never realized how moved she could be by all the little pleading eyes staring back at her.

Pam visited every single kennel. A sense of sorrow suddenly took control of her. Lily was not there. Standing in silence she shook her head. If she had just thought of the idea sooner, if she had just returned to the shelter on Monday, Lily would still have been there. She tried to imagine what kind of family had adopted her. Did they have kids? Were there other cats in the house? She didn't want to believe that Lily had already gotten a home, but she knew deep down inside it shouldn't have come as a surprise to her. Lily was a great kitten.

Before Pam could turn around to leave, a faint meow captured her attention. Looking over her shoulder, two green eyes were staring up at her. Smiling to herself, she walked right up to the kennel.

"Well, look at you!" She reached in between the bars and softly stroked his head.

The little kitten stood up and turned around, purring softly at the gentle touch to his body. Pam instantly noticed his coloring. He was a beautiful shade of gray, just like Lily. He didn't have the white streaks running through his fur like she did, but he did have the same white paws. At close guess he was probably around the same age. With the assistance of a volunteer, the door of the kennel was opened. The little kitten was placed in her arms. The two were face to face. His silky fur felt soft against her arm. His gentle, mellow purring brought a smile to her face. Those two tiny green eyes captured her heart.

"He just went up for adoption today," the volunteer reached over and stroked his head. "We haven't even given him a name yet."

Staring at the kitten, Pam began to rock him back and forth. One paw reached up and pressed against her cheek. Turning to the volunteer, she smiled. "There's no need to give him a name…he already has one."

Sitting in the outer office, the newly-named Grayson sat on Pam's lap purring as if he knew exactly what was happening.

"He sure took to you right away!" Colleen wore the same pleasing smile she always did whenever an animal got adopted.

Reaching down Pam scratched Grayson behind the ears. "He did, didn't he?"

"You made a good choice; he's a great little kitten."

"Honestly I think he is the one who chose me! I actually came here to adopt a different kitten. My boyfriend Joe found a kitten behind the dumpster where he works; we brought her in last week. I was planning on adopting her but she's already gone. I was just getting ready to leave when this one here called out to me."

Pam picked up Grayson and cuddled him in her arms, "This little guy looks a lot like her; he has the same coloring, he just doesn't have the white streaks in his fur like she had."

Colleen set her pen down on the desk, "You said your boyfriend's name was Joe?"

Pam nodded,"Yes."

"And he brought the kitten in last week?"

"Uh-huh, last Saturday."

Colleen immediately stood up,"Come with me."

With Grayson snuggled tightly in her arms, Pam followed Colleen to the back of the building. Colleen opened the door and the two of them walked straight up to Lily's kennel.

"Is this the kitten you were referring to?"

Pam gasped. "Oh my God, it's her! What is she doing back here?"

Lily stood up and quickly approached the front of her kennel... *Hey...I know you!*

"This is the lost and found area. Any animal brought in that was found has to be placed in here for ten days before they can go up for adoption. It's just a waiting period to give those who have owners a chance to find them. She won't be going up for adoption until Wednesday."

A chill instantly shot up the back of Pam's neck,"Joe is going to be so happy! I have to adopt her, I just have to!"

Colleen smiled,"Well, you'll have to come back on Wednesday. We can't even begin the paperwork until then."

"That's fine. I'll be back on Wednesday! I'll be here before you even open!"

Colleen glanced down at Grayson. He looked so happy curled up in her arms. Reaching towards him, she looked up at Pam, "Well, I guess I'll take this guy back to his kennel."

Pam quickly turned around, placing her shoulder in the way of Colleen's arms, "No! He's still going home with me. I'm adopting him today."

Colleen looked surprised. "You're going to adopt both of them?"

"You bet I am."

She glanced back over at Lily, "She is going to be Joe's little kitten."

Pulling Grayson up towards her face, she gently rubbed his fur against her cheek, "This one is going to be mine."

# lily

## A NEW LIFE

We never hang out at Joe's apartment any more. Instead, he's always over here at my place. This is where our family resides. We are one big happy foursome. It will stay this way until Joe and I are married. Then we can all move into the same household and live together. I have witnessed such a change in Joe—a change that I really like. He doesn't look any different; he doesn't act any different; but there is something deep down inside that now shines in his eyes every time I look at them. I see that exact same glow of the eyes every time I look in the mirror.

For two little kittens who did not know each other previously, they get along so well. They are definitely a handful—but that's okay—we love them dearly. They may only be classified as "step" brother and sister, but the bond those two share cannot be measured by any blood line. It's hard to put into words the joy that flows through our hearts when we return home from work, only to be met at the door by two gray balls of fur, running around, sliding across the floor, all in a desperate attempt to gain ownership over the same toy. Watching the two of them at night curl up together before drifting off to sleep brings us both a tremendous sense of peace.

Joe and I will never be able to have children. He knew that when we first started dating. I used to fear that that would be a factor somewhere down the line in our relationship. I no longer have those fears. Joe now has his little girl, and I have Grayson—my little gray son.

# Smokie

## PAIN AND CONFUSION

When Smokie awoke he was staring at a blank wall. *Where am I?* Turning his head slightly to the left he could see a couple of kennels and several of the clinics' staff. *Who are those people?* His mind tried desperately to remember what had happened, but the effort was unsuccessful. The only picture that flashed before him was of tiny, little kibbles lying on the pavement. *Did I get to eat?* He was sure he had. He wasn't at all hungry. He had no idea he was at an animal hospital, no idea that he had been fed intravenously, and he had absolutely no knowledge of the surgery he had just undergone. Feeling pain in his leg, all he could do was wonder where it came from.

"Dr. Matthews…look…he's awake!"

Walking over to the table, Dr. Matthews looked down at Smokie.

"Hey there little boy! Are we feeling a little better?"

Very slowly he ran his hand down the top of his head, just between his eyes. Smokie squinted and managed a faint purr. He liked the way the hand felt against his fur. It was soft and gentle. It kept him from noticing the cast that had been placed around his shaved leg.

Ali walked around to the other side of the table."I'm so glad he made it Dr. Matthews. This one is so special to me."

"Why is that Ali?"

Ali hesitated. Her eyes drifted off into the open space.

"Well I don't usually talk about it, in fact it's been a long time since I've even thought about it...but I was once in this little guy's same shoes. I was walking down the street and I too got hit by a car. Just like with him, the driver never stopped. He just left me lying there and kept on going."

"Oh Ali, I'm so sorry. Did they ever find the person who did it?"

Ali shook her head,"No they didn't. Just like the lady that stopped and brought this little guy to us, a woman saw it happen and came to my aid. She called an ambulance. There were some other people around from what I understand, but I guess they were too busy attending to me to get the license number."

"Well thank God for good Samaritans." Dr. Matthews' voice was sincere. He genuinely liked working with Ali.

"I guess I was unconscious for quite a while. It was weird; I just woke up one day in the hospital. I had no idea what had happened or how I even got there." She glanced down at the table and looked at Smokie, "Just like this little guy."

Late in the afternoon Smokie was ready to be placed in a kennel. Ali stood next to the table and stared at the cast on his leg. A vision of the many stitches, surrounding the metal plate inside, flashed in front of her. Gently she stroked the hair down his back. Closing her eyes, a clear picture of her own scar, the one that ran eleven inches down the back of her leg, quickly came to mind. Opening her eyes, she looked down at Smokie.

"It'll be okay boy," she whispered. "Just like pants cover mine, your fur will grow back and cover it all. No one will ever know it's there."

Letting out a soft purr, Smokie looked straight up into her eyes. He seemed to understand her words.

When Ali arrived the next day for work, she wasn't at all prepared for Dr. Matthews's words. She had been positive the minute Smokie awoke from his surgery that he was going to be just fine, that he was going to be able to lead a normal and happy life. She hadn't anticipated complications from the internal injuries. Smokie would survive, but he would need to be on a very specialized diet. He would have to take medications for the rest of his life.

Ali quickly realized that Smokie was now in need of more than just a home. He was in need of a very special home. She also realized that was going to be a difficult home to find. The only thing that gave her a glimmer of hope for him was the fact that she was a volunteer at the shelter he would be going to after his recovery. She promised him that morning that she would make an extreme effort to find him that special home.

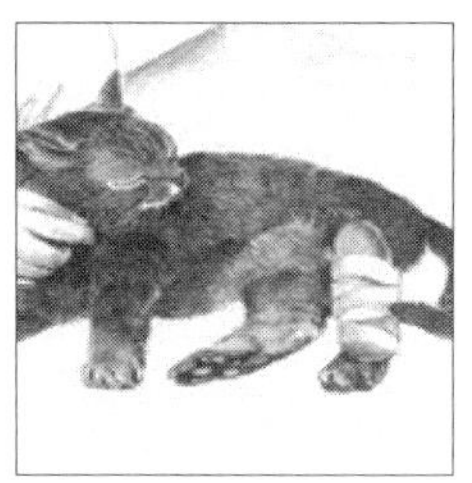

# Smokie

## THE ADOPTION

It wasn't hard for Dr. Matthews to understand the bond that had developed between Smokie and Ali. She had committed herself from day one to being his private nurse. Almost daily, she was down on the floor throwing a ball, waving her hands frantically back and forth, encouraging him to bring it back to her. Sometimes he would hobble towards her, carrying the ball in his mouth; other times he would slowly bat it across the floor until it landed at her feet. Anyone watching from the outside would never know he had a metal rod in his leg, or any internal issues. At a glance he appeared to be just another kitten playing—not a kitten who was undergoing physical therapy.

Ali could not shake her own thoughts of what Smokie had gone through. Every night she went to sleep thinking about him. A kitten lost out in a parking lot, she was sure he had not been alone. She often wondered if he had any brothers or sisters, and allowed her mind to conjure up images of what they would look like. She couldn't help but think that he did. It pained her to think they might have witnessed the accident. Every time visions of him laying on the pavement came to mind, she shuddered. It brought back so many memories.

After a long month of physical therapy and recovery, Smokie was at last ready to be moved to the shelter. Ali was elated that he was ready to seek out a new home, but on the inside she secretly wished the day hadn't come. Thoughts of him leaving the shelter with a new family caused her selfishness to surface. She would never see him again. She would miss him terribly. If only her two cats, Alexis and Athena were not eight and ten years old, she would adopt him in a heartbeat. She had to, however, think of them. Lexi and Athena both liked to do nothing but sleep eighteen hours a day. Their playing days were long over. Snuggling and sleeping was all the two of them cared about. It just wouldn't be fair to them to bring a kitten into their home.

Tuesday evening Ali arrived early at the shelter for her volunteer shift. The first thing on her agenda was to visit Smokie. Lying in his kennel, he stared up at her, his tiny eyes pleading with her to take him out. Rolling his head back, he gently nudged the ball that lay beside him. Ali was sure he wanted to play. Feeling guilty, she blamed herself for the position he was now in—stuck in a kennel all day long. She knew the time they shared together at the animal hospital chasing balls was work, therapy for his leg, but she felt from deep within his eyes, it was nothing more than four wonderful weeks of fun. She reached her fingers in between the bars and gently scratched him behind the ears.

"Aw little boy….I'm so sorry."

Smokie let out a long, soft purr.

Twice a week, on the two nights she volunteered at the shelter, Ali always arrived early to visit him before reporting in. Each time she walked towards his kennel, she anticipated it being empty, but every time she approached it, he stood up to greet her. Her concerns were growing stronger with every encounter. She knew that not everybody would be willing to take on the responsibilities of his care, but she had been confident that someone would. That confidence was slowly starting to fade.

"Why such a long face?" Lisa, her co-volunteer, was quick to notice the change in her demeanor.

"It's the gray kitten we brought in from the hospital three weeks ago." Ali shook her head, "I just can't believe he's still here."

"I know," Lisa agreed. "I thought he would be gone by now too. He's so adorable."

"I just don't understand."

"Well Ali, if it's any consolation, he has had a lot of people look at him."

Ali turned to face her, "Yet no one has adopted him. It's really not that much trouble to give him his medication—it's only once a day! I just can't believe that is what is stopping someone from taking him home!"

"Well, I don't know, the medication may be part of it, but I think it's also the fact that he acts more like a cat than a kitten."

"What do you mean?"

"He doesn't like to play. Everyone who comes in here looking for a kitten is looking for just that—a kitten. They have visions of a little ball of fur running around the house, climbing on things you know, really playful. He isn't into playing at all."

Ali reflected back on his days at the hospital. "During his therapy he chased a ball, even if it wasn't with record speed."

"But you had to coax him right?"

"Well yeah, I guess."

Lisa shook her head, "I don't know if it's due to his injuries or not, but this little guy is never going to be on any track team! He's just as curious as any other kitten, but he is simply not playful at all."

"He still has a lot of great qualities though. Just because he doesn't like to play—just because he's different—is no reason to not want him!"

Ali lay in bed that evening staring up at the ceiling. Alexis and Athena were in their usual spot, curled up right next to her. Gently she stroked the fur on Lexi's back. Smokie would not leave her mind. Visions of his tiny little face appeared everywhere in front of her. Her heart ached for him. She continually pictured in her mind people passing by his kennel, learning of his issues, and then continuing on their way. Suddenly a thought popped into her head. Immediately she sat straight up. Alexis rolled over and looked up at her.

"Oh my gosh, Lexi…how can I judge others for the same mentality I've been plagued with for years?"

Alexis batted her leg with her paw and let out a soft, faint meow.

Ali again stared up at the ceiling. The bond she shared with Smokie suddenly took on a new meaning. Instantly she stretched out, propping herself up on one elbow. She was staring at four adoring eyes that were staring back at her. Athena sat up, reached her two front paws out as far as they would go and arched her back. Three steps and then she sat back down, curling herself up into a ball right next to Ali's side.

"What do you think girl? How would you like to have a little brother?"

Athena looked up at her, and like her sister, allowed a soft, faint meow to be heard, thus giving her approval.

The content sounds of purring echoed throughout the air. Ali rolled over and rested her face against her pillow. A smile found its way onto her lips as she drifted off to sleep.

# smokie

A NEW LIFE

I will never have to wonder how the little gray hospital kitten is doing in life. I see him everyday; he is a permanent member of our household. And, he is no longer referred to as "the little gray kitten." His name is Apollo.

It's amazing to think that his being different from other kittens, a disadvantage in his quest to find a new home, actually turned out to be an advantage. Lisa was right—Apollo will never make the kitty track team—but that is just fine. Alexis and Athena wouldn't have it any other way. A "normal" kitten would have been a disruption to their lives, but Apollo is simply a perfect fit. Every time I watch the three of them all curled up together sharing their kitty dreams, I am completely taken over by a wonderful sense of peace.

I'm sure Apollo will always know what I have done for him...but I don't think he will ever know what he has done for me. I have a brand new outlook on life. Every sunny day, I face the world in a t-shirt and shorts. I no longer dress to hide my scar. It is there…it's permanent…and it does make me different from others. But I have learned, just like Apollo, that difference truly makes no difference at all.

# tasha, tommy and snowball

## SEEKING NEW LIFE

Tommy and Snowball followed their mother's every step. Keeping close behind her, they could not forget the words she spoke as they started out on their journey: *No matter what, we stick together from now on…no one trails off…no one gets lost. This is all that is left of our family…so, no matter what happens…we will not be separated!* They would adhere to her words. Not following the plan was what had caused Lily to get lost, and Smokie to get hit by a car. If the three of them were going to make it, their mom was right, they had to stick together.

The house was far off in the distance. It could no longer be seen. Tommy and Snowball both felt as if they had been traveling for days, but in reality, it had only been a couple of hours. Tasha knew they were tired. Straight ahead she could see hundreds of buildings. They were close to the city streets. Finding a tree with some ruffled leaves at its base, she decided it was time for the two of them to rest, and for her to collect her thoughts. She would need to know which direction she wanted to head once they entered the city.

With her kittens fast asleep, Tasha kept her eyes wide open. Sleep would come for her later, once they had found food and she was sure they were safe. Reflecting back to her life before the house, she remembered the streets she had known so well. Her intention had never been for her kittens to know those streets, but with her dreams of living in the basement of the old house shattered, she had no choice. The streets would offer food.

Early into the darkness of the night, Tommy and Snowball awoke at the exact same moment. Tasha leaned over and licked their heads. *Are you ready?*

Neither one was. Neither wanted to face the uncertainty that lie ahead, but they both stood up and stretched out their paws.

The city streets were lined with hundreds of people. Tommy and Snowball practically pushed up against their mother as she walked as close as she could to the edge of the buildings. They would go a short distance, and then Tasha would quickly dart around a corner, leading them into an alleyway. They would hide out for a brief period of time before venturing back out onto the streets. Snowball was full of fear. She could not help but remember all of the people who were passing by when Smokie got hit by the car. Here on these streets, there were three times as many people and they were all crowded together. Cars continually whizzed back and forth to their left, their headlights flashing in her eyes. She could not help but be afraid of the fate ahead of her.

Tasha finally found a quiet spot. With extreme caution she led them across the street. Tommy and Snowball were sure she had noticed something, but it was her uncanny sense of smell that pulled her in that direction. Behind a small restaurant building she stood next to a dumpster. With one flying leap she was on the edge of it. Looking down at Tommy and Snowball she warned with the fiercest eyes, *Do not move! Stay right here. I will be right back.* The kittens looked around but did not budge. It was quiet. There was no movement around them.

With their hunger finally satisfied, the three of them returned to the streets. Tasha was tired. She had to find a safe place for them so she could get some desperately needed sleep. With her nose high in the air, they had only walked two blocks when she once again darted behind a building. Two huge storage containers stood directly in front of her. Cautiously she approached them. Two dimly lit pole lights gave way for inspection. The place was perfect. There was just enough space between the two side walls for them to easily walk between them, but be totally hidden from view. She could smell the food. In the morning she would figure out a way to get inside. Tonight, they would sleep in peace.

With the creak of the door swinging open, Tasha abruptly awoke. Someone was there. She had to be careful. With the bright sun hovering above them, she feared they might be seen. Creeping along the edge of the metal wall, she slowly poked her head around the side. She didn't even have time to notice the hand clinging to the door. Before she could move, the door had been shut.

"Oh my gosh…look at you!"

Tasha froze. The woman had spotted her.

"Come here, come on, it's okay."

Tasha immediately stepped forward towards the outstretched arm. She had to. If the woman approached her, undoubtedly Tommy and Snowball would be spotted. She had to protect them. Quickly devising a plan, she would allow herself to be picked up. Once in the arms, she would immediately jump and run the other direction. With her fast disappearing act, the woman would surely go on about her business. She would then return to her kittens.

"You are so cute!"

Cradled into a ball, Tasha gave no indication she intended to jump.

"What are you doing out here?" Robin's voice was soft and soothing, but Tasha remained on guard, searching for the perfect moment. "Come on, let's take you inside."

Before turning around, Robin's eyes caught sight of the path between the storage units. Taking three steps forward, she looked in between them. The moment she gasped, Tasha immediately arched her back.

Robin clamped down on Tasha, "No no little girl, it's okay. I'm not going to hurt them."

Turning around she quickly headed for the back door of the building. Tasha squirmed fiercely trying to break free, but Robin had been in this situation before. She knew exactly how to handle her.

"Paige! Paige hurry up, get a kennel!"

Before Robin could get into the room, Paige met her in the hallway with the kennel.

"Where did you find this one?"

"In between the storage units. Here, give me the kennel, I'll put her up, you go outside and get the kittens."

"There are kittens too?"

"Yeah, two of them. They are not back very far, about five feet in between the sheds."

Paige ran back to retrieve another kennel before heading out the back door to find the kittens. Tasha screamed with anger, batting at Robin with both her paws. She knew they were going after Tommy and Snowball.

"It's going to be fine...just calm down." Robin finally got Tasha into the kennel and shut the door. "It's okay, I know you have no idea where you are, but you and your kittens will be perfectly safe here."

Robin was right. Totally unbeknownst to Tasha, she had led her kittens straight into the hands of the local humane society.

# tasha, tommy and snowball

THE ADOPTIONS

The door to the kennel was shut. Tasha glared at Robin with eyes of anger. She was the enemy, but she was a strong enemy. The violent attempts at scratching and the determined squirming to break free had failed. Robin knew instinctively how to handle the situation. With a strong hold of the neck and a tight grip on her legs, she had safely gotten Tasha into a kennel inside the building. Now, watching Robin walk away, Tasha's anger quickly turned to fear as she thought about her kittens. She had no idea what the enemy was going to do to them. Tucking her paws up under her chest, she lay in a guarded position. She would find a way out to the other side of the bars. Waiting with patience, she knew the right moment would come. As soon as someone returned and opened the door, she would catch them off guard. With one flying leap out she would be on the other side. Knowing her kittens had to be somewhere in the same building, she would search for them.

Paige and Robin inspected the kittens thoroughly. Much to their surprise, they both seemed to be in perfect health. After a good cleaning and a very welcomed petting, the two of them each carried one of the kittens snuggly in their arms and returned to Tasha's kennel. Instantly the hard, glaring eyes softened. Tasha immediately stood up. Robin opened the door of the kennel and gently placed one of the kittens inside. Watching it curl right up beside Tasha, Paige followed suit releasing the second kitten, and then slowly closed the door.

With both the kittens by her side, Tasha stared up at the two women with a softened heart. The enemy had turned out to be a friend. The fight had turned out to be a rescue from the streets, not a battle of harm. Consumed by an overwhelming sense of pleasure, she reveled in the joy of their togetherness. Tommy and Snowball stared up at her while she gently licked their heads. That evening she would be able to sleep in peace. Little did she know, this second reunion would be their last. She had no idea, in ten short days, the three of them would be placed up for adoption—separately.

Posted pictures on the shelter's website netted no success in anyone claiming the lost cat and her kittens. Robin had hoped an owner would come forward. She didn't want to see the three of them separated. They were a family; and in her eyes, families needed to stay together. Every day when she brought them food and water, she would take a few moments to watch them. Her mind was full of questions. Was there a family out there somewhere missing her? Had she always been a stray? How long had they been on the streets wandering around? Were these the only two kittens she gave birth to? Staring in silence at the three of them, Robin saw no signs of a tragic ordeal. Knowing it was going to be very hard to separate them when the time came, she wanted Tasha to enjoy her family for as long as she could.

Ten days passed entirely too fast for Robin. With a heart of sadness, she stood in the adoption area staring at the kennels. Placement was important. She would have to move some of the other cats around in order to strategically place the three of them. She wanted to place them apart so that none of them could witness the other being taken away when they found new homes. There was a heaviness tugging at her soul to place the three of them together, all in one kennel, but she knew that was not an option.

"Excuse me..."

Turning around, Robin found herself staring at Nichole.

"Are you who I should see about adopting a cat or a kitten?"

"Uh... yes, I can help you with that. Just let me get these guys into a kennel and I'll be right with you. Feel free to walk around. We have lots of cats—and kittens too— that are up for adoption."

Instinctively Robin walked over to one of the empty kennels and opened up the door. Bending down she pulled Tasha out of the carrier and placed her inside. Barely shutting the door she reached back down to retrieve the kittens. She would leave them together just long enough to assist Nichole, and then she would find a separate kennel for each of them.

Nichole hadn't moved. She remained in place watching Robin's every move. The minute Tasha came into her view; she was instantly attracted to her. A beautiful, black and white Tuxedo cat, followed by two adorable kittens. It was obvious from their looks, the kittens belonged to her.

"That is a gorgeous Tuxedo cat. May I see her?"

Startled, Robin was unaware Nichole was still behind her.

"Oh…uh… yeah, sure."

Reaching back into the kennel, Robin picked up Tasha and handed her to Nichole.

"So you're interested in a cat, not a kitten?"

Nichole wrapped Tasha tightly in her arms. She purred softly at the gentle touch behind her ears.

"Well…" Nichole began with a slight laugh, "That's hard to say. My son Josh wants a cat, not a kitten. My daughter, Meagan, however, wants a kitten, not a cat. I'm hoping the two will somehow find a compromise."

Robin's eyes widened. A glimmer of hope shone in her eyes as the thought popped into her head. If Nichole would consider adopting two of them, her son could have his cat, her daughter could have her kitten, and Tasha would be able to spend her life with at least one of her kittens!

"My husband and I don't really have a preference. It's the kids we can't seem to get to agree."

Robin smiled.

"This one is sure beautiful, and sweet." She glanced over at the kennel. "Are the kittens boys or girls?"

"There's one of each." Robin pointed towards Tommy, "That one is the boy, the other is the girl."

"May I hold one of them?"

"Sure!" Placing Tasha back into the kennel, Robin gently picked up Snowball. "This one is the girl."

Robin could read it in her eyes, Nichole was instantly attached. The timing was perfect. Without hesitation, she offered the little knowledge the shelter had on them, including the manner in which they were discovered out back, hiding between the storage sheds.

"Is it possible to put the two of them on hold…I mean just until this afternoon?"

"Both of them?"

"I just need to bring the kids here to make a decision. I promise I'll be back, just as soon as I pick them up from school."

The shelter did in fact have a twenty-four hour hold policy, but had they not, under the circumstances; Robin would have placed them on hold anyway. Placing Snowball back in the kennel, she had hope. Maybe the kids would not be able to come to an agreement. Maybe Tasha and one of her kittens would go home that afternoon—together.

Four o'clock in the afternoon, Nichole had kept her promise. The Henderson family returned to the shelter. Meagan was ecstatic. Finally, after four months of pleading, the reality of getting a new family member was going to happen. There was no need to look at the other cats or kittens that were available for adoption. Nichole's description of Tasha and Snowball in the car on the ride to the shelter had Meagan already attached to the little girl kitten.

"Oh wow mom, she's cool!" Josh pushed directly in front of his sister,"She looks like she's wearing a tuxedo!"

"Yes she does Josh…that's why she's called a Tuxedo cat."

"She's the one we're getting right?"

Meagan quickly jumped in front of her brother,"No we're not. We're getting the kitten!"

With her hands placed firmly on the kennel, Meagan pressed her face up against the bars,"Mommy I want to hold the little girl kitten!"

Robin smiled at Nichole,"Would you like me to get them both out for you?"

Nichole shook her head,"Yes that would be great. Josh can hold the cat and Meagan can hold the kitten. Maybe then the two of them can make a decision."

Meagan squealed with delight as she wrapped Snowball up in her arms. "Mommy, I want this one."

"No," Josh commanded,"We're getting the cat." Tasha's fur was pressed firmly against his face. "Listen to her purr…"

"This one is purring too!"

Tommy stood up and approached the front of the kennel. His soft meow cried out for attention. Mr. Henderson glanced his way, and then looked directly at his wife. She was staring hard at Tommy.

"Mom, I want this one!"

Staying true to her nature, Meagan could not possibly agree with her brother, "No mommy I want this one. Let's get the kitten!"

Nichole glanced over her shoulder, looking straight up at her husband. She didn't even have to say a word.

"I know, I know," he whispered, "They're never going to agree. I guess they'll just each have to have their own."

Nichole broke out into a wide smile.

Kneeling down on one knee, Mr. Henderson looked directly at his two children, "Alright kids, this is what we're going to do. You each have to promise that you will take good care of them; give them a lot of love and attention, but you also have to promise to take on the responsibility of cleaning their litter box and feeding them."

"I will daddy, I promise!"

"Me too, dad!"

"Okay. I expect you to hold up your end of the bargain. In return for your promise, you each can have the one you want."

"Yippee! You're going home with us!" Meagan twirled Snowball around in the air.

Josh gave Tasha a warm, close hug.

Robin's face lit up with gleam. "You're going to adopt both of them?"

Mr. Henderson stood up and faced his wife. She was still smiling, but there seemed to be a sadness in her eyes. She was staring again at Tommy. With raised eyebrows he glanced over at the tiny face behind the bars, then at his wife, and then back at the tiny face. He almost felt as if the two of them were somehow communicating. Tommy instantly noticed the new set of eyes upon him.

*Take me with you! You don't understand—mom, Snowball and I made a pact. We would not be separated, under any circumstances! You can't take them and leave me behind!*

Instantly he rubbed his cheek up and down on the bars. His meow echoed in Mr. Henderson's ears. He looked again at his wife.

"Nichole…you okay?"

Nodding her head she kept her voice low, "Yes…I'm fine. It's just kind of sad. They were a family just like us, and now we're going to split them apart."

Reaching over he wrapped his arms tightly around her. Her compassion had always been one of the qualities he adored about his wife. He gently pressed his lips up to her ear.

"I suppose you want a kitten of your very own, huh?" he whispered.

With pleading eyes, she raised her head and looked directly at him.

Slowly turning his attention back to Robin, Mr. Henderson finally answered her question, "Actually, no. We're not going to adopt the both of them...we're going to adopt all three of them."

# tasha, tommy and snowball

NEW LIVES

I don't think if I had written a tale about our family cat and her kittens, I could have come up with an ending better than the one we currently live with. Adopting a family of felines was certainly not our intention. It was however, the best thing we've ever done. The lessons learned from this experience will stay with us forever. Meagan and Josh have definitely kept their promise, and that promise has instilled in them a new sense of responsibility. Not only do they take great care of their pets, they now help out around the house with a sense of pride. No longer do I have to ask for assistance with the chores. The two of them readily volunteer before my request can be made. Even my husband, before curling up at night on the couch with our little threesome, lends a hand to the tasks that need to be done.

As for me, I too have learned a valuable lesson. Before the three of them came into our household, I was at a point of dissatisfaction with my life. After college, I chose to not seek a career but instead to start a family. Now, with the kids in school all day, doubts about whether or not I was fulfilling my true potential in life were beginning to set in. I was no longer feeling important, no longer feeling special. These days, my thoughts are totally different.

If the four of us never knew the importance of animals in this world before, we certainly do now. Watching our cat nurturing her young brings home the importance of family. When I look at her, I see a very special mom—the same thing I now see when I look in the mirror. We kept her family together, and she has brought ours closer. Sometimes saving a life can create a new one of your very own.

# tasha, tommy and snowball

MEAGAN'S WORDS

You know, I bugged my mom for almost four months to buy me a kitten. She just kept pushing the subject off, telling me she was not going to "buy" us any kind of pet. She talked about responsibility and being ready, but I always thought it had to do with money—although she never did say that. The day she picked us up from school and we went to the shelter, I was absolutely shocked when she told me and Josh that we were going to adopt all three of them! I could not believe my ears! The adoption fee for each one of the kittens was ninety dollars, and it was seventy dollars for the cat! Later that evening I asked her why she refused to buy me a kitten when I had originally asked. Before I let her answer, I made sure to remind her that she had just spent two hundred and fifty dollars, and I was quick to inform her that we would have come out so much cheaper had she just bought a kitten in the first place. This was her answer:

"Honey, it's not about how many dollars we spent. Yes, we could have bought a kitten for less money…but we would not have, in any way, come out cheaper. By adopting the three of these guys….our lives are going to be so much richer!"

I totally didn't understand her words that day…but I certainly do now.

# jelly and justin

CHAPTER THREE

# jelly and justin

ANOTHER RIDE

The ride was a long one. Jelly and Justin lay in their kennels across from each other. The two of them were going to the same shelter, although neither of them knew it. They both believed they were merely passing friends.

Jelly stared hard at Justin. She had been in this predicament once before, in a van, on the way to a shelter, but something seemed different this time. The quietness of the engine made her think—a lot. Would things ever be different? Would she ever find herself in a position where she could just find a home and stay? She had always felt safe in the abandoned building she once called home. Sure it was tough, scrounging the streets every day for food, but at least there she had had stability. She knew where she would lay her head every night—off in a corner against a concrete brick, amongst all of her friends. There she had security. Back then she had been sure that would be her home forever.

Justin rolled over and let out a soft meow. Tilting his head, he found himself looking directly at Jelly. He was a bit shy—never having found any stability or trust in his lifetime, but he couldn't help but notice the way she was looking at him.

*Hi, my name is Jelly. What's your name?*

*Jelly? Did you say Jelly?*

*Yeah, I know it's kind of weird, but I once had an owner who gave me that name.*

Justin stretched out his paws and then sat up in his kennel. He inched his way close up to the bars.

*Why did they name you Jelly?*

*Well...Mrs. Brown—Amanda—had two sons. They were the people who came to the shelter and adopted me. Before them my name was Bridgette, but they changed it. Anyway, her sons loved to eat peanut butter and jelly sandwiches, so they wanted to name me Peanut Butter and Jelly. Amanda told them the name was way too long so they shortened it to P. Jelly. But they never called me that, they just called me Jelly.*

*Wow, that's pretty interesting.*

*So what is your name?*

*I'm Justin. I don't have a fascinating story to tell about my name. I've never had an owner, just the shelters. One of the volunteers at the shelter—I don't even know which shelter it was—gave me that name.*

*You've never had an owner or a home? Wow, how many shelters have you been in?*

*The one I'm going to now will be my third.*

Jelly instantly felt ashamed. In her lifetime, at least she had had two homes, the abandoned building with her alley cat friends, and the one with the Browns. She felt a twinge of guilt for her brief moment of doubt. Deep down inside she knew she would find another home. How sad for Justin, he had not even had one.

*How old are you Justin?*

*I'll be five months old next month.*

*And this will be your third shelter?* Jelly was clearly shocked. *Why don't you just stay in one place? Maybe then you'd be able to find a home.*

*I can't, they won't let me. The two shelters I've been in are not what they call a "no kill" shelter. I'm not really sure what that means, but I know it has something to do with why I keep getting moved around. Whatever it is, it must be something bad. On a certain day towards the end of the month I hear my time is up, and then someone scrambles around to find another place to send me.*

*I'm so sorry Justin. If you could just get into a home…life would be a lot different.*

Jelly reflected back to Amanda and the boys. She knew they didn't want to have to give her away. It wasn't Amanda's fault her new military orders were taking her out of the country. It was one thing to take the boys to a foreign country, but a cat was something different. There were enough tears shed around their household before they left for Jelly to know, without a doubt, she would really be missed—and always remembered.

Justin looked at her with skepticism, *If life was so great in a home, then why are you here?*

Closing her eyes, Jelly envisioned Amanda setting a plate of food down in front of her. She could see the boys flying in the front door after school, dropping their books down on the floor and dashing into the living room to find her.

*Circumstances Justin…just circumstances.* Slowly she opened her eyes. *They did not want to give me away, but they were chartering into unknown territory. Moving to another country, Amanda was very worried about how the people over there would view animals and she was concerned with what the stress would do to me. She talked to me a lot Justin; she shed a lot of tears.*

Justin said nothing. He just stared at her.

*Their hearts were in the right place…they really did have my best interest in mind.*

Justin wanted to believe her words, but that was a very difficult task for him. He had heard words all the time, from the volunteers at the shelters, but there wasn't any real "communication" between him and them. He got a lot of attention, they spoke soft words to him, petted him and played with him, but he never shared with anyone that connection that Jelly was talking about. There just always seemed to be a distance there—one that was not measurable by any metrics. He wanted to understand Jelly's optimism; but he had yet to be given the chance in life to see things from a positive viewpoint.

The van suddenly rolled to a stop. Justin and Jelly both sat straight up. Glancing at the back of the van, the doors suddenly opened. Justin looked over at Jelly.

*I guess this is where we say good-bye. That's too bad. I would have liked to have gotten to know you better.*

Jelly did not have time to respond. Two hands reached into the van. Both kennels were picked up. With Jelly on the man's left side and Justin on his right, they tried to peer at each other through the bars. Justin could clearly read the words "animal shelter" as they entered into the building. There was no mistaking them—he knew them all too well.

Both kennels were placed on the floor by the man's feet. Jelly wished he would have set them down so she and Justin could face each other. Meeting a new friend excited her. Realizing they were both being taken to the same shelter, she felt sure Justin's friendship would help comfort her loss of Amanda and the boys. More importantly, she felt that he needed her. With a little effort, she could help him see things in a positive light. She would be the one to restore the faith she was sure he must have had at one time; that one day he would get a good, loving home.

Jelly had only spent two days at the shelter Amanda had originally taken her to before being transported to the new facility she was now in. She had no idea that the first shelter had been completely full and, she had only been accepted with the agreement that she would have to be transported elsewhere. In her eyes, whatever had happened was fate. She was supposed to be in that van, riding down that road. She was meant to have met Justin.

The journey had been a long one. Jelly and Justin were both tired. Lying in their kennels, they were ecstatic that they had been placed at an angle, right next to each other. Wearing silent smiles they closed their eyes and drifted off to sleep. Daylight would bring plenty of time to talk.

Jelly was the first of the two to awake. Stretching out her paws, she stared up towards the ceiling. Tilting her head sideways, her eyes caught sight of Justin. He was still sound asleep.

*Justin...wake up. It's morning!*

One eye slowly opened. *It's awfully early Jelly.*

*No it's not. Come on wake up.*

Justin almost turned a back flip as he rolled over and fully opened his eyes. He didn't really want to get up, but Jelly's pleas warmed his heart. It was uncanny how fond of her he had become in such a short period of time. If she wanted to get up and talk, that was the least he could do to make her happy.

*You know since we both came from shelters already, we'll probably go up for adoption really fast. We could soon be separated, so we have to make the most of what little time we have together now.*

Justin stared at her. He had just met her, and having instantly taken a liking to her, he couldn't bear to think about not seeing her ever again, not so soon. The thought of her already becoming just another memory made him cringe.

*Let's not talk about that Jelly.*

*Okay, so what do you want to talk about?*

*Tell me what it was like to have an owner. Tell me about your life before you met Amanda and the boys.*

Jelly smiled. Fond memories rolled into her mind. Flashing across her brainwaves were visions—visions of Amanda, the boys, and her own mother.

*Well, let's see...my grandmother's name was Buttons. She lived with the Lawson family. I never met her, but from what my mother has told me...the Lawsons loved her dearly. She was treated like royalty and spoiled rotten. There were never any bad moments in her life, at least not until the time she got pregnant. The Lawsons weren't very happy about that. She had four kittens—my mother, two other girls and a boy. The Lawsons gave away the two girls and the boy and kept only my mother.*

Jelly suddenly stopped her words. Momentarily she stared off into space. *Somewhere out there Justin, I have two aunts and an uncle whom I've never even met.*

Justin stared at her in confusion. He wasn't really sure exactly what an aunt or an uncle was, but he could tell from the way Jelly spoke, they must be important people.

Snapping back into reality, Jelly continued with her story.

*My mother lived with my grandmother for several years before my grandmother passed away. She too enjoyed the rich life—living with owners who really loved and cared for her. Only about a year after my grandmother passed on, the Lawsons decided to move. My mother heard them say they were moving into a nursing home. She wasn't sure what that was, but she told me she heard Mrs. Lawson say that they didn't accept cats. She got scared. She was totally unsure what was going to happen to her, so she just took off one day.*

*She just ran away and didn't know where she was going to go?*

*Yep. She just took off. A couple of days later she decided to return to see if the Lawsons were still there, but they weren't. They were already gone.*

*So what did your mom do then?*

*That's when she became what I've heard people call a "street cat." She sort of just roamed the streets. She hooked up with a group of homeless cats and lived in an abandoned building on the east side of town.*

*Wow. That's incredible!*

*That's where I was born. We may not have had owners, but we sure did have a lot of friends. Everyone always seemed to help each other out and take care of each other. Someone always seemed to be able to find food, and the one thing that everyone did was share. None of us ever went without food when one of us had it.*

*So the abandoned building was where you grew up? Where is your mother now? Do you have any brothers or sisters?*

*Boy you sure are full of questions, Justin. I am an only cat, no brothers or sisters that I know of. My mother…unfortunately…was killed by a car while trying to cross the street.*

Justin could not only hear the choking of her voice with her last statement, he could see the tears well up in her eyes.

*I know in my heart it was an accident Justin, truly it was. The guy didn't mean to hit her…but the sad thing was he did nothing about it. He stopped his car, got out and looked at her, then got back into his car and drove away. He didn't even go up to her to see if she was still alive, or try to help her. He did absolutely nothing. He just got into his car and drove away like she meant nothing to the world.*

Tears were now streaming down her face. *She may have meant nothing to the world, Justin…but she meant everything to me!*

*Oh Jelly…I'm so sorry.*

*I was only three months old! It just wasn't fair.*

Justin desperately wanted to get out of his kennel and crawl up next to her in hers. His heart ached for her pain. He knew she appreciated him being there to listen, but he felt as if that wasn't enough. He so wanted to go over to her and give her a great big hug.

Jelly returned to her silence. Gently closing her eyes, her heart could feel a long distance attachment to her mother's soul. She knew her mother was listening. She knew her mother could sense her pain from far away.

Justin felt he had to offer his words of five-month-old wisdom—something he hadn't known he had ever had—until he met Jelly.

*Jelly…I am so sorry for your loss, but you know what? You are a very special cat. You have been through so much in your life…and you have handled it so well. A lot of cats do not ever find themselves faced with the tragedies you have suffered. You have faced your own obstacles with such a positive attitude. You seem to look to the good in life, no matter the bad that has come your way. I, for one, admire you greatly for that.*

Jelly turned to stare at him. She had not even realized how much she had opened herself up to him, but she was instantly glad she did. For a kitten that had not even begun to live the experiences she had already gone through, he seemed to understand perfectly. A smile gently swept across her face.

*You know Justin…I admire you as well. You are pretty darn wise for a kitten!*

His meow revealed his laughter.

With a new, light-hearted view, Jelly finished her story. She told Justin how all of the alley cats banded together like one huge family, taking wonderful care of her for almost nine months after the loss of her mother, until animal control discovered the abandoned building where they lived. She relived her experiences at the first shelter she found herself in, and then recounted her life with the two-legged creatures of the world—Amanda and the boys.

*So what about you Justin? What has your life been like? Did you ever know your mother or your father?*

Justin was not as eager to speak, but there had already developed a sense of trust between the two of them. His story was not as fascinating, but it did hold its own merit.

*I never even knew my father, and I have very vague memories of my mother. As far as I know she never had a home with owners. I was born on the streets—just like you. We lived in the subways…but we didn't have any friends. I don't really know what happened to her. We were out looking for food one day, I turned around and she just wasn't there. I called out for her, went looking everywhere I could think of, but I couldn't find her anywhere. We just somehow got separated.*

*Justin I'm so sorry. It must have been so hard on you not knowing what happened to her!*

*I went back to the subway, thinking maybe she would show up. She never did.*

*So how did you end up in the shelter?*

*Just like you…animal control. I went out the next morning to search for her and then all of the sudden I was picked up by this man and put into a van. That's when the shelters became my home.*

Jelly shook her head. *You are such a great kitten; I just can't believe no one would have adopted you, especially with all the time you've spent in shelters!*

*There was always so much competition there. There were so many of us...mom and dad cats, but a lot of kittens too! It's so hard to believe that there are that many of us out there who need homes, but, let me tell you—I have discovered there are! Oh, I've had people interested in me before, but it always seemed that the kittens with a known history are the first to go. When one of the volunteers could say that it was an unexpected litter...or they knew of the person who brought the kitten to the shelter, people seemed to believe that that would guarantee a well-mannered animal. Those of us whose past was unknown always seemed to be the last ones to get people to take us.*

Jelly sat back in her kennel, away from the bars. She didn't want Justin to see her tears. How sad for him. Such a great, wise kitten. No one knew. No one had ever given him the chance.

*Sometimes Justin...people just don't realize what they are missing out on when they prejudge. But you know what? One day things will be different. I know. I believe! One day there won't be any more of us homeless, unwanted animals. It may take a while, but I know deep in my heart, one day it will happen. One day people will understand.*

*You really think so Jelly?*

*All you have to do Justin...is believe. That's what they call faith. Without it, life doesn't matter anyway!*

Justin rolled over and stretched out his paws. He adored her words. He wasn't sure if they would ever come true or not, but just the positive energy of her spirit made him happy. Faith! What a great concept. If it kept her in that good of spirits, it was something he could definitely use in his life. Instantly he made a promise to himself—faith—it was something he would definitely work on. He would practice it, believe it, and he would keep it close to his heart.

# jelly and justin

HAVING FAITH

True to Jelly's prediction, she and Justin were placed up for adoption within a matter of days. Although Jelly was on the other side of the room, she was directly across from Justin. He could easily see her by merely lifting his head. Every time the two of them looked at each other, they both carried a silent smile—one that no one could understand—except for them. Justin lay in his kennel with a completely new outlook. Somehow he knew that this would be the last shelter he would ever see. He wasn't sure how he knew it, but somewhere deep down inside his heart, he knew. Curling up at the back of his kennel, for the first time in his life, he felt content.

Jelly was the first one to find a new owner. Justin watched from his kennel as Nora held her close to her heart.

"She's absolutely beautiful!" she told the volunteer, "And, she's so mellow. I just know this is going to be a match made in heaven!"

Jelly let out a loud meow as Nora began to walk away, still holding her in her arms.

"What little girl? What is it?"

Jelly was looking straight across the room at Justin. Nora glanced in his direction, "Is that your friend? Do you want to say good-bye?"

Jelly looked directly into Nora's eyes. She wasn't sure that the message that was transpiring, but Nora could definitely read something in those eyes.

"Okay little girl, we'll go say good-bye!"

Gently stroking her fur, Nora carried Jelly over to Justin's kennel. In total amazement, she stood perfectly still, watching the two of them stare deep into each other's eyes. Something she had never before seen in her life was happening. There were no meows, no purrs, nothing. There was only a serene, quiet silence, but Nora had no doubt the two of them were somehow communicating.

*Justin…this is where we say good-bye. I'm going home now, with Nora. It is a sad moment for the two of us…but yet at the same time, it is a happy moment. It is a new beginning. I know…I believe…you will be right behind me. In my heart I know your new owner is right beyond those doors.*

*You know what Jelly? You're right. For the first time in my life I feel no sadness. I have faith. Somehow I know that this is the last shelter I will ever see…and I know that because I have met you. You have given me a gift that is beyond words, beyond any price tag life can place on anything. You have given me hope. I can do nothing more than wish you a wonderful life in your new home. I do not feel that this is good-bye for us. Somehow I know one day, we'll meet again.*

Both eyes quickly diverted from each other. Jelly looked up at Nora.

Nora instantly felt a strange chill shoot up her spine, "Are you ready now sweet angel?"

A soft meow emerged. *Yes Nora, I'm ready now. Thank you.*

Jelly looked back over Nora's shoulder as the two of them exited the room. Locking eyes with Justin for the last time, the air carried a very silent message—*I love you Justin.*

To many it may have seemed like an eternity, but for Justin, it felt like only a matter of minutes. After only three weeks of being at his new shelter, he found the new owners he believed he would one day find. It only took little Brandy one glance, and she was hooked. Justin stared down at her with a wide smile and big, curious eyes. He had never really paid attention to the little people of the world, but her long brown hair and short, petite stature peaked his curiosity. He walked right up to the bars of his kennel.

"Mommy, mommy, I want him!"

Her mother quickly appeared by her side, "Honey, we haven't even really looked around yet. You can't know this fast that you want this particular one."

Brandy stared up at her mother with the biggest, brownest eyes, "Yes, I can mommy. He spoke to me! He said he wanted to come home with us!"

Jeanette stared down at her daughter. Just as always, those big, pleading eyes sucked her heart right in.

"Don't you want to see the other kittens they have?"

The hair shaking fiercely back and forth gave the answer the words truly didn't need to speak,"NO! I want to take him home! He wants us, I can tell!"

Justin let out a soft meow, rubbing his face against the bars.

Glancing over at the volunteer, Jeanette shook her head,"Who can argue with the logic of a child?"

She looked over at Justin and smiled,"I guess we'll be adopting this one."

# jelly and justin

## JELLY'S NEW LIFE

Nora was awakened by the soft feel of fur brushing up against her cheek. One gentle purr in her ear told her it was time to get up. With closed eyes, she rolled over and scratched Jelly behind the ear, "Okay little girl, we'll get up."

Jelly was already pacing back and forth on the counter when Nora appeared in the kitchen. With a burst of laughter at the morning dance she witnessed every day, Nora placed food and fresh water in the bowls, and then set them down on the floor. Jelly immediately jumped down.

After showering Nora headed back downstairs. Jelly was in her usual spot, sitting quietly by the glass sliding door.

"Okay Jelly, but remember you only have about an hour okay? I'm driving up to the mountains today with Jill. You have to be in the house while I'm gone."

Jelly meowed softly, almost as if telling Nora she understood the allotted time frame. The door was opened. Jelly slid out onto the patio. Nora watched her momentarily as she walked across the yard before returning upstairs to get dressed.

The doorbell rang just as Nora was pouring her second cup of coffee of the morning.

"Come on in Jill, the door is open."

Laying her bag against the hallway wall, Jill joined Nora in the kitchen. She was poured a cup of coffee and the two of them went into the dining room.

"Where's Jelly?"

"She's outside. Oh don't worry; she'll come back in before we leave."

Jill showed her skepticism, "Yeah? How can you be so sure?"

Nora set her coffee cup down on the table, pulled out a chair and sat down. She was smiling.

"Jelly really is a strange cat. Do you remember when I first got her a couple of months ago? I told you then I was never going to let her outside."

"Yes, I remember that Nora, but you certainly didn't hold true to that statement!"

"Well...I gave in because she would constantly sit at the door, crying to get out. I don't know, I guess in her previous life she was outdoors a lot. I felt so guilty keeping her locked inside; knowing she was most likely accustomed to the outside. The first time I let her out, I stayed with her, constantly watching her like a hawk. I was totally ready to pounce on her the minute she tried to jump the fence. But she just never did. She merely roamed around the backyard. It was almost like she was perfectly content being outside, but perfectly content in her new home. I know now that she has no intention of leaving."

"You have no fears that one day she may see something and just take off?"

Nora shook her head, "Absolutely not. We have a very unique bond and understanding of each other. It's almost sort of weird!"

Nora stood up, "Come here, let me show you something."

The two of them walked over to the glass sliding door. Jill was almost shocked to see Jelly sitting with another cat on a wooden corner ledge that had been built into the fence.

"You let her sit on that ledge?"

Nora smiled and nodded. "Not only do I allow her to sit on that ledge, I actually built that ledge for her!"

"Are you nuts?"

"No I'm not. I just know my cat, and she knows me. She trusts me to provide for her and take care of her, and I trust her that she won't leave me. Like I told you, we have a very unique and special bond. I had to give her some of what I think is her past, so that she would know I understand her. She has proven to me that my theory is a good one, day after day."

"Okay…so you let her out in the backyard…but why build her that ledge? That only gives her better sight to a lot of things surrounding the area. It also gives her an advantage to easily jump over the fence!"

Nora laughed, "Jill, even without the ledge, she can easily jump that fence."

"So…back to my question, why did you build the corner ledge?"

Looking back out through the sliding glass door, Nora pointed to her neighbor's house, the one on the backside of the fence they shared, "See that house? I'm sure that's their cat sitting on the ledge with Jelly. I've actually never spoken to them, but their cat and my Jelly sure talk to each other all the time."

"What do you mean?"

"Well their cat is obviously allowed outdoors a lot because many times I have seen it in my backyard with Jelly. The only two times I have looked out this door and haven't seen Jelly, I immediately darted outside and ran up to the fence. Sure enough Jelly was in their backyard with their cat!"

Nora started laughing, "It's almost like the two are neighbor cats who like to meet in the afternoon to have their cup of tea!"

"So, you built the ledge to act as their tea table?"

Nora shook her head, "Something like that. I built it so the two of them could spend time together. It's amazing how they seem to have bonded. It's a lot more comfortable for them than sitting on the fence post. Jelly only gets to go out in the backyard twice a day, once in the morning before I go to work and then in the afternoon when I get home. During the day and at night she is indoors with me. Every afternoon when I let her out, she goes right to that ledge. Within minutes the neighbor's cat joins her. You should see the two of them laying on that ledge, curled up together and basking in the sunlight. It is the perfect picture!"

Jill turned around to head into the kitchen to refill her coffee.

"Whatever you say Nora."

Nora looked down at her watch, "Wow, we really should get going." Without paying any attention to Jill, she opened up the sliding glass door.

"Jelly, come on. It's time to go! You can see your buddy tomorrow!"

Jelly immediately jumped off of the ledge.

Jill turned around just in time to watch Jelly walk right back through the glass sliding door and into the house. Looking over at Jill, she let out a soft meow. With only seven steps, she walked right over to her bed next to the couch and curled up. Gently, she closed her eyes.

# jelly and justin

## JUSTIN'S NEW LIFE

"Mom, I'm going to let Justin out!" Brandy, her hand firmly attached to the glass sliding door, did not wait for her mother's response. With one hard pull the door was open. Justin was immediately on the other side. Pulling the door closed, she stood quietly and watched him for several minutes. Justin ventured out into the backyard. Slow steps, one by one, his head was raised in the air. His eyes were searching.

"Don't worry little boy," Brandy whispered, "She'll come."

"How do you get your cat to do that?" Sally, Brandy's new friend was intrigued.

"Do what?"

"Stay in the back yard like that. Did you train him?"

Brandy laughed,"No, I think he actually trained us."

"What do you mean?"

"When we first brought him home, he would sit at the door and meow at the top of his lungs. One day mom and I took him outside to play in the backyard. We figured if we went out with him, he wouldn't run away. He loves being outside! Sure enough, he proved us right. He showed us that if we would let him out, he would not leave. My mom says it's because he knows we rescued him. We have a very special connection, a certain sense of trust."

"I'm going to ask my parents if we can get a cat."

"Well if they say yes, just be sure to adopt one. Adopted cats make awesome pets. Come on; let's go up to my room."

Justin wandered around the yard for several minutes before finding a nice spot off in the corner. Curling up on a small patch of grass, he closed his eyes and lifted his head to the sky. The rays of the sun beat down on him gently, warming his entire body. A soft meow emerged, although no one could hear it.

The sliding glass door at the next door neighbor's house suddenly shut. Justin stretched out his paws, yawned, and then rested his chin on his paws. Sure enough, Buffy's nose appeared between the small layers of cracks in the wooden fence. Seeing Justin, she let out three loud barks. Justin opened his eyes, and slowly turned his head in her direction.

*Hey, Buffy.*

*Come on Justin, hop the fence. Let's play*

Justin got up and slowly treaded over to the fence, stopping every now and then to completely stretch out his body. Buffy laughed with amusement. Sitting down directly in front of the fence, Justin batted his paw through the crack, gently touching her nose.

*I need to stay within view today. Brandy has a friend over. They'll be coming outside soon to play.*

Buffy let out a sigh, *Okay. But it's a beautiful day. You gotta come over later okay?*

*Okay Buffy.*

Buffy roamed around her backyard, entertaining herself by chasing a ball. Her efforts lasted a mere ten minutes. It really was a beautiful day, the kind of day for just lying around and being lazy. Unlike humans who found the bright, breezy days perfect for biking, hiking and doing all sorts of activities, she was just like so many of her four-legged friends—she could find unique pleasure in reveling in the sunshine and doing absolutely nothing. Strolling over to the corner of her yard, she slowly approached her dog house. Curling up next to it, she repeated the same actions that Justin was doing in his own yard, stretching out her paws, and then gently resting her chin upon them. The warmth of the sun gave her a sense of peace and tranquility. Shutting her eyes, she slowly drifted off to sleep.

In his own backyard, amidst the tranquil peace, Justin heard the meow. One eye quickly opened.

*Pssst…Hey Justin. I'm here!*

Justin immediately jumped up. Two beautiful blue eyes were staring at him. Walking up to the edge of the back of the fence, he took one flying leap. Within an instant, he was on the ledge.

*Hi Jelly!*

*I don't have a lot of time today. Nora is going on a ski trip. Right now she's getting ready.*

*That's okay. Brandy has a friend over and I'm sure they'll be out soon to play.*

*It's a gorgeous day.*

*I know—I was so enjoying the sunlight.*

Jelly curled herself up into a ball. Justin lay down next to her, brushing up against her fur.

*Isn't it funny how fate works Justin?*

Justin tilted his head back towards her and smiled.

*It really is Jelly. All you have to do is have faith…and believe. I once knew this ter-*

*rific cat who taught me that!*

Jelly smiled. Purring softly she moved closer to Justin. Together, they both slowly closed their eyes and let the heat of the sun warm the moment.

# CHAPTER FOUR

# May

UNEXPECTED SURPRISE

May sat on her window sill perch. The day was perfect. The sun was shining brightly, complimented by several white blankets of cotton floating amidst the beautiful blue background of the sky. Even through the glass pane, she could feel its warmth.

Staring out the window she remained perfectly quiet—not a purr, not a meow, not even the sound of her own heart beating could be heard. Pebbles lay quietly on the floor watching her. She wanted to join her on the perch, but something told her not to. May was in that deep trance again. She was in her own little world. Pebbles desperately wanted to know what it was that had captured her attention out that window. This was now the third week in a row that May had found it necessary to retreat to that perch just underneath the window and stare out into the day for hours on end. Something had to have happened in the neighborhood. Something only she could understand. Pebbles had jumped up on the perch many times when May wasn't around; staring out the window, moving her head from side to side. She never saw one thing out of the ordinary. Every thing was the same, week after week—dogs in their yards, cats roaming the neighborhood—nothing had changed. No new neighbors had moved in. No new fences had gone up. There may have been a couple extra cats and dogs joining the neighborhood scene, but that had happened many times in the past. It had never been the cause for any alarm.

Forest treaded into the "cat room." Walking up to Pebbles, he lay down next to her.

*May staring out that window again?* His whisper was almost sympathetic.

Pebbles glanced over at him, *Yeah,* she sighed. *I wish I knew what it was that has her so captivated! Something out there seems to fascinate her, but she won't tell anybody what it is!*

*Give her more time Pebbles. We're close knit around here, you know that. May will come around in her own time—when she's ready. For now we just need to be there to support her, with whatever she needs. If that need is time, we have to give it to her.*

*I guess you're right Forest. I just wish there was something I could do for her.*

*There is...just be there for her when the time comes. She'll confide in us when she's ready. That's what family is all about.*

May stayed on her perch in the window sill for almost an hour. Suddenly she jumped down, went downstairs and walked into the kitchen. Without saying a word, she ate from her bowl, then walked into the living room and curled up underneath the coffee table.

Forest and Pebbles watched her go without saying a word. Mira suddenly appeared in the room, instantly taking up space on the cat couch. Forest got up and walked over to the tallest condominium in the room. With one flying leap, he perched himself on the top of it. Pebbles moved over to the corner and lay down in one of the four cat beds on the floor.

*Where's May?* Mira was the first to speak.

*She went into the kitchen to eat.*

*Was she on the window sill perch again?*

Pebbles sighed, *yeah, she was.*

Mira lay her head down on her paws. *What do you think it is guys? What has happened in the neighborhood in the past month to make her act the way she has? Has anyone been able to figure out why she constantly sits on that perch and stares out the window?*

*There are a few more cats and two new dogs in the neighborhood but that's nothing abnormal. Other than that, I can't see anything different.*

*Neither can I*, Forest added.

Mira looked at them with a deep stare. She thought for a brief moment before speaking, *Okay...if there's nothing else abnormal in the neighborhood, then she has to be taken by either one of the new cats or dogs that have moved in. That has to be the answer!*

*Okay,* Pebbles was the first to remark, *but why now? We've had lots of new animal neighbors move in in the past.*

*Well obviously there's something different about one of the recent newcomers!*

*So how do we get her to talk about it?*

*I told you Pebbles, we don't. We let her bring it up when she's ready.*

*I disagree Forest,* Mira pronounced, *I think we need to bring the matter up. Whatever it is she probably feels alone. We need to let her know we're here for her.*

Pebbles looked over at Forest, but did not comment.

Mira continued. *We have to approach the subject with caution—somehow we have to let her know that we are here to support her, but that we are not going to force the issue. We just need to let her know that we know something is going on, and that we will support her no matter what it is. We need to let her know that when she is ready to share her thoughts, we'll be there.*

With the three of them in total agreement, they all went about their ways. Forest stretched out to take a nap. Pebbles jumped off her cat bed and ran over to the circus tent to play with the attached toys. Mira remained on the cat couch, quietly awaiting opportunity to arise. It knocked faster than she had anticipated. Before any of them had time to drift off to sleep, May entered the cat room again. They all stared at her. The air was silent.

*Okay guys…what's going on? Why the silent treatment?*

Mira, the eldest of the group, looked around at Pebbles and Forest, and then back at May. She knew she was to be the spokesperson—it was in her age.

With troubled eyes, she turned her attention to May.

*May…we know something is going on with you. We are not sure what, but we know something is. We're just concerned for you. None of us wants to push you to talk about it; we just want you to know that we are here for you. Whatever you want to say we will listen.*

May instantly sat down. She hadn't been aware her actions had been noticed. She looked around at her siblings. Although adopted ones, they were just as real and special as any true brother or sister could be. She knew she had to open up to them. It would only be right to share her latest joys with them.

*Come on guys…I want to show you something.*

The three of them watched her walk immediately over to the window sill and jump up on the perch. Moving over to the far left of it, she motioned for them to join her. They all did.

May stared out the window. A hint of a smile appeared on her face, *Do you see that fence…the one four houses away? The one that has the ledge built into the corner of it?*

Forest, Mira and Pebbles all stared out in that direction. Forest was the first to reply, *Yeah, I see it.*

May glanced at him with admiring eyes, and then turned her attention back to the empty ledge. *There's a new cat in the neighborhood, I've watched him day after day. He lives at that house—the one that shares the fence with the other house. Everyday he comes out of his house and joins the cat that lives at the adjacent house on that ledge. They just sit there for hours on end. I'm not sure what they talk about and on many days I have seen them just curl up together and sleep.*

Pebbles looked at her with confusion. *Does that make you want to be able to go outside, May?*

*Oh no Pebbles, not at all.*

Pebbles looked again at the ledge. *But May, if it's not wanting to be on the outside then what is it? They don't share anything we don't. We're all a family and we have each other. We curl up and sleep together. What is so special about him?*

*No, Pebbles…it isn't that. They share nothing that we don't, believe me. It's just… it's just that before I came and joined this household…I had a life as a "street cat."*

Pebbles tilted her head. *Was he a "street cat?" Can you tell? Is that what's wrong—you miss that life?*

*Oh no Pebbles, I don't miss that life style at all! I would never trade this wonderful, loving house for the life I had in the past. In those days I never dreamed I would have an owner who would love me, care for me and take care of me. Back then, I thought the streets would be my life. I never knew one day I would have such great brothers and sisters like all of you.*

*But you do May, you have that great life now, and you have us. So what is it about that cat that interests you so much? Do you recognize him? Did you know him in your previous life?*

May again looked out the window at that ledge. Then she turned to face her two sisters and her brother.

*Have any of you looked out this window and seen those two cats together?*

Pebbles was hesitant about answering. She didn't want May to think she had been spying on her.

*Uh…I have.*

*You have Pebbles? You have sat on this window perch and seen the cat that lives at the house sharing the fence?*

Instantly she lowered her head, *Uh…yes May…I have.*

*Then you, Pebbles…you have seen my son.*

Mira, Forest and Pebbles all looked at each other. They were completely stunned.

*What?*

*That cat, the little male, he is my son.*

*Your son? We didn't even know you had a son. How can you be so sure May? How can you know he is your son?*

May smiled an innermost, comforting, peaceful smile. *A mother just knows, Pebbles.*

The three of them instantly edged closer to her. Curling up together they all brushed up against her fur. *Tell us May…tell us what happened.*

*Well...back when I was a street cat, I gave birth to three kittens. Neither one of my daughters made it. My son, Hailey…was the only one who survived. We lived together in the subways…just him and I. One day we were out looking for food on the streets and I was suddenly picked up by animal control. They didn't see Hailey, at least at the time, I didn't think they did. He wasn't put in the van with me. I was taken to the shelter alone. I had no idea what happened to him.*

*That was the same shelter we all came from right?*

*Yes, the same shelter. I remember when Cathy was talking to the volunteer that day, the day she brought me home. She was saying how much she adored all of you, and that I would make a nice addition to the family. Holding me in her arms, she told that volunteer that she never knew how great a household could be when a person adopted animals. She felt a special bond with all of you…and that it was amazing how anyone could not want the animals that had enriched her life so greatly. She actually said all of the love you had provided for her simply could not be measured by words.*

*She really said that?*

*Oh yes…and I believe now, even more than the day she held me in her arms ready to take me home, that she meant it.*

*So...you were happy when she brought you here right?* Forest had to ask the question. He clearly remembered that day. When Cathy had brought May home, the three of them had been very excited at the new addition, but even with her first steps, May had proven to be extremely cautious.

*Actually Forest, I wasn't sure what to think. I never knew what it was like to have food at my feet the minute I was hungry, what it was like to have my fur stroked and I'd never had the pleasure of a two legged creature rolling around on the floor, trying to get me to chase a mouse! Once more, I had certainly never heard of a cat room!*

The three of them looked at her with adoring eyes. They all had their stories of doubt to tell before coming into Cathy's home. None of them had ever been on the streets, but Forest had been shifted around, having had two prior homes. Mira had been physically abused by her previous owner, and little Pebbles lived in a home where she was treated as nothing more than a statue, a bundle of fur just starving for love and attention.

*I missed Hailey terribly and I didn't like being confined to a kennel. I remember sitting alone and thinking about him, wondering where he was and if he was okay.*

*That must have been torture for you.*

May glanced over at Pebbles, *In a way yes, but somehow I had a certain sense of peace. It's like I knew in my heart that he was going to be okay. It wasn't easy, but I kept my faith that everything was going to work out just fine.*

*And it did, huh May? You met Cathy. You now have her and us!*

May smiled, *Yes it did Pebbles…yes it did.*

*Humans are the best thing in the world when you hook up with the right one!*

*You are so right Forest—and true brothers and sisters do not have to come from the same blood lines!*

Mira instantly perked up her ears. *Look May. There he is! He just came outside.*

All of them stared out the window. Justin stretched out on the lawn, his eyes peering up at the ledge.

A warm fire suddenly ignited in May's heart. A peaceful, content smile swept across her lips.

*Do you wish you could talk to him May?*

May did not take her eyes off of her son. *We have different lives now Mira. He has a good life, he is happy. I can tell. It is enough for me to know that he has friends and a loving family who will take care of him. That is what is important.*

Mira brushed her face up against May's fur.

*Besides, in my heart I know that one day…one day he will be sitting on that ledge and he will look over in our direction. The minute he sees me in this window, just like the moment I laid eyes on him, he will know exactly who I am.*

# rainbow bridge

Just this side of heaven is a place called Rainbow Bridge.

When an animal dies that has been especially close to someone here, that pet goes to Rainbow Bridge. There are meadows and hills for all of our special friends so they can run and play together. There is plenty of food, water, and sunshine so that our friends are warm and comfortable.

All the animals that had been ill and old are restored to health and vigor. Those who were hurt or maimed are made whole and strong again, just as we remember them in our dreams of days and times gone by. The animals are happy and content, except for one small thing—they each miss someone very special to them, someone who had to be left behind.

They all run and play together, but eventually the day comes when one of the animals suddenly stops and looks into the distance. His bright eyes are intent.

His eager body quivers. Suddenly he begins to run from the group, flying over the green grass, his legs carrying him faster and faster.

You have been spotted, and when you and your special friend finally meet, you cling together in joyous reunion, never to be parted again. The happy kisses rain upon your face; your hands again caress his beloved head; and, you look once more into the trusting eyes of your pet, so long gone from your life, but never absent from your heart.

Then, you cross Rainbow Bridge together…

Original Author—Unknown

# a call to action

The perception of animals as "pets" has come a long way over the years. In fact, in many households today, animals are no longer viewed as simply "pets"—they are viewed as family members. They ride with us in our cars on errands, they share our beds, and they even receive gifts at holidays.

Considering our recent shift in perspective, there is one question that calls out to those who care enough to listen and are willing to take action. This question is as powerful as it is profound and it is something that I believe every person in America should ask themselves. It is this question that inspires books such as this one and challenges readers to pay attention to the world around them. The question? **How is it possible that we, as a nation, allow breeders to sell thousands of cats to pet stores each day, when simultaneously thousands of cats are euthanized simply because shelters are unable to find homes for these unwanted pets?**

Baffling, isn't it? So, how can *you* help? When making the decision to bring an animal into your home, think first about saving a life—Think Adoption First! Your simple, yet empowering choice to open your heart and home to an animal in need, truly can make a difference. You can also help by making a donation to the animal charity of your choice or volunteering in your spare time to help out at a shelter.

# resources

In addition to the following list of resources, please visit **www.dnjbooks.com** for additional links and helpful resources to support you in making the decision to save a life.

## National Animal Organizations

**American Society for the Prevention of Cruelty to Animals (ASPCA)**
424 E. 92nd Street
New York, New York 10128-6804
(212) 876-7700
***www.aspca.org***

The ASPCA was founded in 1866 as the first humane organization in the Western Hemisphere. The Society was formed to alleviate the injustices animals faced then, and we continue to battle cruelty today. Whether it's saving a pet who has been accidentally poisoned, fighting to pass humane laws, rescuing animals from abuse or sharing resources with shelters across the country, we work toward the day in which no animal will live in pain or fear.

**Best Friends Sanctuary**
5001 Angel Canyon Road
Kanab, Utah 84741-5000
(435) 644-2001
***www.bestfriends.org***

Best Friends is working with you—and with humane groups all across the country -- to bring about a time when there are No More Homeless Pets. Best Friends reaches across the nation, helping humane groups, individual people, and entire communities to set up spay/neuter, shelter, foster, and adoption programs in their own neighborhoods, cities, and states.

**Alley Cat Rescue (ACR)**
The National Cat Protection Association
P.O. Box 585
Mt. Rainier, MD 20712
(301) 277-5595
***www.saveacat.org***

Alley Cat Rescue (ACR) works to protect cats on several levels: locally through rescue, rehabilitation and adoption of cats and nationally through a network of Cat Action Teams. ACR is dedicated to the health, well-being and welfare of all cats: domestic, stray, abandoned and feral. ACR also assists the international animal community.

**The Humane Society of the United States (HSUS)**
2100 L Street, NW
Washington, D.C. 20037
(202) 452-1100
***www.hsus.org***

The Humane Society of the United States is the nation's largest and most effective animal protection organization—backed by 10 million Americans, or one in every 30. Established in 1954, The HSUS seeks a humane and sustainable world for all animals—a world that will also benefit people. HSUS is America's mainstream force against cruelty, exploitation and neglect, as well as the most trusted voice extolling the human-animal bond.

**Pets911.com**
Finding home for our nation's pets
***www.pets911.com***

PETS 911 believes that if you consolidate all the adoption, lost and found, veterinarian/emergency clinic, fostering, volunteer, shelter/clinic, and health and training information out there and give the public a single and easy place to find this information; education will substantially increase and euthanasia will decrease. That is our mission.

**Petfinder.com**
***www.petfinder.com***

The temporary home of 250,000 adoptable pets from 10,000 adoption groups.

+++

## Animal Organizations in Colorado

**Colorado Humane Society (CHS)**
2760 South Platte River Drive
Englewood, Colorado 80110
(303) 781-9344
***www.coloradohumane.org***

Colorado Humane is Colorado's only open admission shelter where no clock is ticking. As an open-door shelter, no animal is turned away. With no clock ticking, CHS does not euthanize for money or space considerations. It is relatively easy to accomplish one of these goals, but to stand firm for both is a Herculean task. This is what sets us apart from every other organization in Colorado.

**Denver Dumb Friends League**
2080 South Quebec Street
Denver, Colorado 80231
(303) 751-5772
***www.ddfl.org***

Founded in 1910, the Dumb Friends League is a national leader in providing humane care to lost and abandoned animals, rescuing sick, injured and abused animals, adopting pets to new homes, helping pets stay in homes, and educating pet owners and the public about the needs of companion animals.

The Dumb Friends League is the largest animal welfare organization in the Rocky Mountain region, welcoming tens of thousands animals to our two shelters. We turn no animals away.

**MaxFund**
1025 Galapago Street
Denver, Colorado 80204
(303) 595-4917
***www.maxfund.org***

The MaxFund is a TRUE no-kill shelter. There is no pre-sorting of animals into "adoptable" and "non-adoptable" categories, discarding the so-called "unadoptable." The MaxFund takes every animal it has the space for. EVERY animal is kept until its owner is found or it is placed in a new adoptive home. The only reason for euthanasia is when it is in the humane interest of the animal.

**Table Mountain Animal Center (TMAC)**
4105 Youngfield Service Road
Golden, Colorado 80401
(303) 278-7575
***www.tablemountainanimals.org***

Table Mountain Animal Center's Mission is to provide the best CARE possible for every animal that enters our doors.

+++

## Additional Resources and Information

**HomeAgain®**

"Always looking out for your pet."

1-888-HOMEAGAIN (1-888-466-3242)

***http://www.homeagain.com***

You may think that your pet is protected from getting lost. But accidents happen, and some things – like hurricanes and other natural disasters – are out of your control. In fact, one in three pets will become lost during their lifetime. And according to the American Humane Association, only about 17 percent of lost dogs and two percent of lost cats ever find their way back to their original owners. Almost 4 million pets are euthanized every year because their owners can't be found in time if a shelter cannot determine a pet's owner or medical history, the pet may be euthanized in as few as three days. To help give your pet the best chance of being identified should he ever become lost, have him implanted with the HomeAgain microchip.

**Poison Control**

Call (888) 426-4435

***http://www.aspca.org***

As the premier animal poison control center in North America, the APCC is your best resource for any animal poison-related emergency, 24 hours a day, 365 days a year. If you think that your pet may have ingested a potentially poisonous substance, make the call that can make all the difference.

+++

If you have a special fondness for a particular breed, there are many breed-specific rescue groups that operate through foster homes to rescue animals. You can find these groups locally through most search engines.